Ju

Chri

work and vocation

David Field and
Elspeth Stephenson

Inter-Varsity Press

INTER-VARSITY PRESS
Universities and Colleges Christian Fellowship
38 De Montfort Street, Leicester LE1 7GP
© DAVID FIELD AND ELSPETH STEPHENSON, 1978
ISBN 0 85110 403 7
Biblical quotations are from the
Revised Standard Version,
copyrighted 1946 and 1952,
unless otherwise stated.
Set in 10-11 Garamond
Printed in Great Britain by
Hunt Barnard Printing Ltd.,
Aylesbury, Bucks.

Contents

¹This chapter appeared previously, under the title *Work*, in *Taking sides*, published by IVP, 1975.

Preface

This book has been written for those who are seriously interested in formulating their own Christian view of work and vocation. It consists of a package and twelve pieces of unpacking.

The package is a chapter by David Field, director of studies and lecturer in ethics at Oak Hill College, London. The theme is work; what the Bible has to say about it and how the Bible's principles may apply to those of us who live in the last quarter of the twentieth century.

The unpacking was done by thirteen Christians who read the chapter and agreed to tell us about their own experience of work and vocation in the light of what they had read. To help with the unpacking Elspeth Stephenson, a freelance broadcaster, interviewed most of the contributors and most of the book consists of tidied-up transcripts of those interviews. Chapters 6 and 7 were written in the usual way.

The result is twelve chapters of great variety. The contributors were chosen because they were in widely differing jobs. They belong to different denominations. Their personalities differ. But above all it became clear as the chapters came together that God deals with each of his servants individually. Within the framework of the truth about God and man as revealed in the Bible (a framework described by some critics as a strait-jacket) there is room for God to guide each of his servants on individual and differing paths.

The danger of variety in a book of this kind is that it may cause confusion. Personal experiences are always interesting, but if we believe that God guides each of us individually we cannot transpose someone else's guidance and experience and use it as our own. To get full value from the book the reader must participate, thinking through his own response to David Field's chapter and following up the study questions at the end of each chapter. In this way, principles can be absorbed and their implications appreciated by the individual. Better still, discussion groups could use the questions as a basis for their meetings.

What is work?

'Work' is notoriously difficult to define. To a pre-school aged child 'working' is a delight; it is imitating what mummy and daddy do. The delight usually continues into school, but as the years pass 'work' is redefined as 'what you are told to do'. Leisure is everything else. Then, often after the acute drudgery of exams, we leave school and 'go to work'. Now 'work' is what you're paid to do and evening study is suddenly part of your leisure activities.

Children often define work as what they dislike doing. Leisure is then equated with pleasure and is the opposite of work. Some adults don't get much beyond this, but some actually enjoy their work. So perhaps work is that which I am paid to do? But what do we say of the office clerk who enjoys an easy life at 'work' and is paid for it and who spends every evening forcing himself to the threshold of pain in a gym or on the running track as an amateur athlete? Or the church voluntary 'worker' who does more in her spare time than in her 'work'? Or the housewife of whom it is said that 'she never goes to work'? Or the executive who exhausts himself in an armchair all day 'merely' thinking?

In the end perhaps we can get no further than the good old

dictionary definition, 'work, *n.* application of effort to a purpose'.

In this book, the word 'work' will appear many times and with a number of different shades of meaning. To avoid confusion it would be well to bear this in mind.

Guidance

This is not a book about guidance, but the reader who sees a job as a calling will want to know, 'How do I hear the call of God?', 'How can I be sure that I am called?' A booklet that has helped thousands is *Guidance* by Oliver Barclay, published by IVP (fifth edition, 1978).

Part 1: The package

1

Work, the Bible and you
David Field

'A Christian young lady of fortune', suggests one of George Eliot's characters in *Middlemarch*, 'should find her ideal of life in village charities, patronage of the humbler clergy, the perusal of Female Scripture Characters ... and the care of her soul over her embroidery in her boudoir – with a background of prospective marriage to a man who – if less strict than herself, as being involved in *affairs religiously inexplicable* – might be prayed for, and seasonably exhorted.'[1]

Middlemarch is, of course, a period piece, set in days long before organized labour and Women's Lib. appeared on the industrial scene, but the description of a Monday-to-Friday job as an 'affair religiously inexplicable' (the italics are mine) is not wholly out of tune with the attitude some Christians adopt towards their daily work. A job is seen simply as the long, dull tunnel that separates Sundays, which are the *Lord's* days when his work can be done. Discussion of major social issues, such as the merits of alternative economic systems or the problems of industrial relations, seems vaguely unspiritual – the kind of thing, in fact, that can thankfully be left to the politicians.

This is admittedly only a caricature. There are many Christians who do see their daily jobs as important outlets for serving God, and an increasing number who are becoming seriously involved in attempts to apply Christian insights to the complex problems posed by a highly industrialized society. Those who secretly regard such efforts as a waste of valuable time which might be spent more profitably in a mid-week church activity may themselves be surprised to discover just

[1] G. Eliot, *Middlemarch* (Chatto, 1950).

how much Scripture has to say about work and working relationships. Conditions of work in Bible times were, of course, very different from those of today, which means that the greatest care must be taken in carrying biblical teaching across the time and culture gap of so many centuries, but there are important basic principles in the Bible which remain relevant to man's working life in this or any other age.

The Bible and work

1. A God who works

The Bible's doctrine of God sets the scene for the very high view of work that Scripture presents. With great daring, the Old Testament writers describe God as a manual labourer, working with his hands and fingers to make the world. He is the Potter, elbow-deep in clay (Isaiah 45:9). The whole of creation is 'the work of his hands' (Psalm 8:3, 6), and, like any worker, he has his rest day (Genesis 2:2, 3). He even experiences deep job-satisfaction (Genesis 1:31).

Some religious thinkers in Bible times found the idea of a working God abhorrent. They invented a 'demiurge', a semi-divine clerk of works whose job it was to supervise the messy business of bringing the world into being, so the Supreme Being (as they thought) would not have to dirty his hands with the nuts and bolts of creation. In strong contrast, the Genesis creation account has no room for any demiurge. The God of the Bible is a God who works.

Jesus, too, described his main life-purpose in working terms. Towards the beginning of his ministry, when his disciples urged him to stop for a meal, he replied, 'My food is to do the will of him who sent me, and to accomplish his work' (John 4:34). And nearing the end of his life he could say to his Father in prayer, 'I glorified thee on earth, having accomplished the work which thou gavest me to do' (John 17:4).

Jesus' main life-work was, of course, absolutely unique – the work of redemption – but he was also a working man in the more normal, everyday sense. His contemporaries knew him as the carpenter of Nazareth (Mark 6:3), and in New Testament times carpentry was a physically demanding trade. There was no works store down the Nazareth High Street to supply a convenient piece of three-by-two on demand. In all probability, a joiner in Jesus' day would have had to cut and fetch his own timber before starting to make a table or chair (without, of course, the aid of power-tools). And it was in this muscle-building trade that Jesus spent all but three years of his working life. The hands which held the whip that drove the crooked money-changers from the temple in Jerusalem had been hardened by years of work with an axe, a saw and a hammer. Tough, physical labour was not beneath the dignity of the Son of God.

2. Working man

Against this backcloth of a working God, it is hardly surprising to find Scripture taking a very high view of the dignity of human labour. The first chapters of Genesis make it quite plain that work was part of God's ideal creation plan for mankind from the very beginning. Adam was instructed to 'till and keep' the Garden of Eden (Genesis 2:15), a combination of agricultural labour and estate management which must have added up to a most demanding job. Earlier still, the very first command God gave to man included an order to work (Genesis 1:28), and there is an important sense in which the modern nuclear physicist, the explorer, and the man on the production line are still fulfilling those primeval instructions from the Creator to 'fill the earth and subdue it'. From a Christian point of view, it is by no means naïve to say that God continues his work of sustaining creation today through man's labour. One only has to list the numbers of those involved in the food trade, for example, from the growing of raw materials in the fields to the packaging of goods and service in the shops, to realize just how much human work is involved in answering the simple prayer, 'Give us this day our daily bread.' This was something the Reformers saw very clearly. 'God even milks the cows through you,' insisted Martin Luther.[2]

It is therefore quite wrong to see work as a side-effect of human sin, something invented by the Devil to ruin man's leisurely enjoyment of God's world. The Bible certainly teaches us that man's fall into sin spoiled working conditions (in Genesis 3, for the first time, we are told that the ground resisted Adam's efforts to work it), but the arrival of sin could do nothing to negate God's creation ideal. Man was created in the image of a working God, and work is as natural to him as sunset is to day (Psalm 104:19, 23).

In the last book of the Bible, there may even be a hint that the value of the work we do now will not be lost in heaven. Those who 'die in the Lord', we are told, will 'rest from their *labours*' (an umbrella term for all the unpleasant and painful aspects of toil which are a legacy from the Fall), but 'their *works* follow them' (Revelation 14:13, AV). Dr Leon Morris's comments on this verse are worth repeating: 'Heaven is not so much a place where no work is done as one where pain has ceased. The believer rests from his *labours*, but his *works* go into the life beyond the grave. This gives dignity to all the work in which Christian men engage. They are occupied in no insignificant task.'[3] The dream of a workless paradise is clearly not a vision of heaven.

The Bible, then, shows us a working God who has made man to be a worker too. Fitting the pieces together, three practical conclusions emerge.

In the first place, *it is bad for man to refuse work.* This is a conclusion the Bible itself underlines in both Old and New Testaments. 'If anyone will not work,' writes Paul with brutal bluntness, 'let him not eat' (2 Thessalonians 3:10). The book of Proverbs is rather more colourful: 'Go to the ant, O sluggard; consider her ways, and be wise' (Proverbs 6:6). Scripture has no time for idlers.

Secondly, on the same grounds, *it must be wrong to deprive a*

[2] Quoted by C. F. H. Henry, *Aspects of Christian Social Ethics* (Eerdmans, 1964), p. 43.
[3] L. Morris, Tyndale Commentary on *Revelation* (IVP, 1969), p. 183.

man of work. Because God intended man to be a worker, to deny any fit person the opportunity of employment is to rob him of something essential to his full humanity. Even social security payments, however generous, are inadequate compensation for enforced unemployment, because the welfare state's charity is no substitute for the contribution God intends a working man to make towards the upkeep and improvement of his society. As William Temple wrote, referring to the unemployed in Jarrow in the slump of the '20s and '30s, 'The gravest and bitterest injury of their state is not the animal grievance of hunger or discomfort, nor even the mental grievance of vacuity and boredom; it is the spiritual grievance of being allowed no opportunity of contributing to the general life and welfare of the community.'[4] Television documentaries on unemployment in Northern Ireland bear striking witness to the truth of Temple's words. The listlessness and sadness on the faces in the dole queue testify to the emptiness of life without work.

Then, thirdly and positively, it follows from the biblical teaching that *work has a very high value*. It is at this point especially that the Christian finds himself in conflict with those whose life-style assumes that work is something inevitably oppressive and burdensome. 'If the daily job is no longer the most time-*consuming* aspect of human existence,' suggested Carl Henry, when editor of the American periodical *Christianity Today*, 'it has nonetheless for countless thousands become life's most time-*oppressive* factor.'[5] The way some advertisements are worded shows that this is no exaggeration. When a job is advertised, it is comparatively rarely that any stress is laid on the work involved, especially if this is likely to be strenuous or arduous. The spotlight may fall on the size of the salary (payable at the end of a week's work); the amount of annual holiday (to be taken as a break from work); the extent of sickness benefits (when the applicant is too sick to work); or the size of the pension (to be paid when he is too old to work); on anything, in fact, but the job itself and the work it demands.

Advertisers both reflect and reinforce the spirit of the age,

[4] F. A. Iremonger, *William Temple* (OUP, 1948), p. 440.
[5] C. F. H. Henry, *Aspects of Christian Social Ethics*, p. 32.

and naturally it is difficult for an individual to resist their pressure. Nevertheless, an attitude of mind which looks upon work as man's supreme indignity (little more than an unfortunately necessary means to a pay-packet or salary-cheque) is clearly out of line with Scripture. The fact that God works, invests all work with dignity. And the fact that he created man to work, invests all work with normality. To look forward longingly to the time when we need work only a one-day week, or put our feet up on the mantelpiece and do no work at all, is not only sub-Christian thinking; according to the Bible, it is sub-*human* too.

Personal attitudes

All that has been said so far threads its way back to the Bible's account of man's creation, as a worker, in the image of the working God. There is an important sense, therefore, in which creation teaching speaks to all men, whether or not they have found faith in Jesus Christ. But there is also a considerable body of biblical teaching which is directed specifically to the Christian, setting out a distinctively Christian approach to work.

1. Vocation

First and foremost, according to the Bible, *every Christian has a vocation*. There is a great deal of misunderstanding on this score. Fastened to the wall in the central square of a well-known theological college are several notice-boards, on which the names of college prize-winners are inscribed in gold lettering. Until recently, one of those boards was reserved for the names of past students who had gone overseas to serve as missionaries. That board has now been removed and taken elsewhere, not because overseas interest in the college has waned, but because it was very wisely recognized that a list of missionaries is out of place in a roll-call of prize-winners. Nevertheless, the attitude to Christian vocation which caused the board to be put there in the first place, still survives in the church.

The tendency to catalogue jobs in some kind of spiritual football league table is deeply engrained on the Christian mind. Way out at the top of the list come those who have 'vocations' – including, no doubt, missionaries and clergy, followed at a short distance by RE teachers, doctors and nurses. Halfway down, we meet those with 'ordinary jobs' (such as businessmen, electrical engineers and secretaries who do not work for Christian organizations). Then, right at the bottom, and in serious danger of relegation, are those involved in much more dubious pursuits – pop musicians, perhaps (unless they subscribe to *Buzz*), and barmaids.

This division of jobs into vocations and 'others' is quite foreign to Scripture. The Bible's approach to work assumes that every man should have a job, and that every Christian, whatever his job, has a vocation. Vocation, after all, only means 'calling'. Indeed, we cramp the style of Scripture cruelly if we confine the meaning of vocation to our week-day employment. Every Christian is called by God to *do* something with his life, and to *be* something for him. When Paul wrote to the church at Ephesus, he was only too well aware that he was addressing a very mixed crowd of converts. In the congregation there were employers and ex-thieves, housewives and children, as well as slaves (which, as we shall see, was a term that covered a broad spectrum of working people). Yet, in spite of this widely-divergent range of occupations, he was able to say to all his readers, 'I therefore, a prisoner for the Lord, beg you to lead a life worthy of the calling to which you have been called' (Ephesians 4:1).

In another of his letters, Paul compares the shameless jostling for key jobs in the church to a state of civil war among the limbs and organs of the body. He points out that it is the smaller and often neglected parts which perform some of the most vital functions (1 Corinthians 12). If it is within the spirit of Scripture to extend the force of this teaching to all work – Monday to Friday as well as Sunday – the Christian must beware of falling into the trap of valuing one occupation above another. Using Paul's analogy, to exalt the 'spiritual' work of the missionary over the 'secular' work of the plumber is really to say that the tongue is more important than the kidneys. As far as the Christian is concerned, all jobs can be sacred (when they are done in obedience to God's will), and all are secular (because they are worked out in the world).

Every Christian has a vocation. That much is plain from the Bible. But what is equally clear is that a Christian's vocation cannot be limited artificially to his trade or profession. If it is, then the shortening of the working week becomes something of an embarrassment. How, it may be asked, is a Christian on a three-day week to view his vocation, when he spends more time away from his job than he does doing it?

One answer suggested by an American writer is that he should look for his life's calling in out-of-work activities. That, however, would be a most inadequate solution. To regard one's bread-and-butter job as a mere make-weight results, as we have seen, in a sub-Christian view of work. It might also lead some Christians into a state of frustration and even breakdown, if increasing responsibilities at the office make the idea of a three-day week, in their cases, rather a poor kind of joke. This is a stress that many Christian businessmen experience now. As the pressures at work grow, week-day church activities are either skimped or abandoned, and if out-of-work activities have come to be regarded as the main focus of vocation, it is not hard to imagine what heart-searching and tension may result.

The biblical answer (as is clear from Ephesians 4:1) is that God's calling cannot be tied down to any particular activity. Vocation extends to all hours, as well as to all jobs. The balance between so-called 'working' and 'non-working' hours may differ between individuals; it will probably also vary in the individual's own experience from time to time. But no Christian (providing he is living faithfully) can ever step outside the boundaries of his vocation. So to fret over time spent at an office desk which might have been devoted to a church Bible class may be to misunderstand the all-embracing scope of God's calling.

2. Motivation

Inevitably, if a man is convinced that he has a vocation from God, his motivation for work will be deeply affected, too.

The experts are divided as to exactly what makes people work harder. The profit motive, which might seem to provide the main stimulus, is usually played down nowadays. J. A. C. Brown, for example, writes: 'Without exception, all industrial psychologists are agreed that money is of much less significance than has hitherto been supposed. Except under conditions when wages are very low or during periods of inflation, money is one of the least powerful incentives.'[6] Even with this proviso, the ordinary working man might be allowed an incredulous whistle at that, but it is nevertheless true that other powerful factors, besides money, do influence our approach to work. Prospects of promotion spur some, while the promise of more leisure time attracts others. Even the call of job-satisfaction is not altogether a voice from the past.

For the Christian with a vocation, however, there is one overriding incentive. Above everything else, he does his work to please God. In the New Testament it is Paul who sets out the consequences of this unique source of motivation most clearly. 'Work heartily,' he tells Christian slaves at Colossae, 'as serving the Lord and not men' (Colossians 3:23). After issuing a similar instruction to slaves in the congregation at Ephesus, he amplifies it a little: ' . . . not in the way of eye-service, as men-pleasers, but as servants of Christ, doing the will of God from the heart, rendering service with a good will as to the Lord and not to men' (Ephesians 6:6, 7).

Workers with a sense of vocation are inevitably men and women with ambition. Whole-heartedness demands that no Christian can simply relax as soon as he has mastered his job or collected enough capital to retire comfortably. God's calling drives him to the limits of his physical and mental capacities. 'Oh to be nothing!' can never, therefore, be a Christian's prayer. To be sure, an overwhelming desire to please Christ is

[6] J. A. C. Brown, *The Social Psychology of Industry* (Penguin, 1954), pp. 201f.

quite distinct from any self-seeking incentive, but in practical terms the results may be much the same. In most firms, hard work, however motivated, brings added responsibility, which in turn normally means promotion. One of the reasons (though only one) why so few Christians are to be found in unskilled jobs may well be that Christian commitment stretches capabilities and opens up new horizons. As Carl Henry provocatively observes, 'to turn a screw with Job-like patience on an assembly line is no reproach if it represents one's highest level of creative ability. Such limitation is sinful, however, for a disciple of Christ who has greater potential for service.'[7]

Mention of work on an assembly line, however, raises one powerful objection. Modern working conditions are patently very different from those of Bible times. A Ford welfare-worker tells of a revealing conversation he once had with a man on the assembly line in a Detroit factory:

'What are you making?' he asked.
'C429,' came the bored reply.
'What is C429?'
'I don't know.'
'What becomes of C429 when it leaves you?'
'I don't know.'
'How long have you been making C429?'
'Nine years.'[8]

Is it not simply naïve, he asked, looking back on this exchange, to demand of anyone – even the most ardent Christian – that he should spend nine whole-hearted years making a C429? Even a slave in Bible times could work creatively; he was at least near enough to the finished product to be able to take a pride in his job. But standing in front of a machine that stamps out brackets for forty-two hours a week can hardly be called 'creative' by any stretch of the imagination.

Hard though it may be, this is an objection the Christian is bound to resist. If he is on the management side, of course, he has a responsibility to relieve the boredom of others and to

[7] C. F. H. Henry, *Aspects of Christian Social Ethics*, p. 61.
[8] Quoted by S. Cave, *The Christian Way* (Nisbet, 1949), p. 207.

heighten their job-satisfaction.[9] But even if he is powerless to make changes, uncongenial conditions cannot rob the Christian worker of his unique incentive. Paul's all-embracing command to 'work heartily' was written to slaves, and anyone who imagines that a slave at Colossae was the ancient counterpart of a mellow eighteenth-century English craftsman should have his rose-tinted spectacles removed. Not every slave-master was kind and gentle (*cf.* 1 Peter 2:18). Most regarded their slave-labour as just another part of the over-all plant, which an efficient employer would renew at regular intervals. One Roman farming handbook[1] divided agricultural implements into three categories – the 'mute' (meaning the farm vehicles), the 'inarticulate' (the animals), and the 'articulate' (the slaves); and it was the author's advice that a new man just taking over an estate should make it his very first job to go round and throw out all the inefficient tools in each category – mute or articulate. When to this is added the fact that most white- and blue-collar workers were slaves in New Testament times (including doctors, teachers and accountants), Paul's instructions become all the more remarkable.

All too often the slave's working conditions were far from congenial, and he had no security against instant redundancy. Nor is the contrast between creative work and routine monotony one that we find stressed in Scripture. If anything, the Bible views so-called 'creative' work with some suspicion, because admiration of 'the work of men's hands' could so easily lead to idolatry (*cf.* Psalm 115:4; Isaiah 40:19). On balance, therefore, the Christian is not entitled to plead, 'Give me the right conditions – *then* I will work whole-heartedly.'

Social issues

If conditions of work were frequently oppressive, it is puzzling to find so little criticism in the New Testament of the social environment in which slavery flourished. Why did

[9] For the responsibilities of management, see further on pp. 28ff.
[1] Varro (116–27 BC), *De Re Rustica*.

Paul content himself with giving advice to masters and slaves on the way they should behave towards one another, when instead he might have aimed a broadside against the institution of slavery itself? The Bible disappoints many radicals by its apparently kid-gloved approach to the corrupt institutions of society. Jesus, says his critics, did not go nearly far enough in his fight for social justice. He had a great many compassionate things to say to the deprived and downtrodden. He also had some sharp words for the representatives of the selfish rich, and for members of the hypocritical religious establishment. But he *did* virtually nothing to change the social environment in which all the unfairness and suffering flourished.

The criticism has spilled over into modern times. Professor Tawney, for example, scorning the church's timidity in soft-pedalling the problems of industrial conflict, concludes that Christians 'relieved the wounded and comforted the dying but they dared not enter the battle'.[2]

Brian Wren tells a modern parable with the same message.[3] 'There was once a factory which employed thousands of people. Its production line was a miracle of modern engineering, turning out thousands of machines every day. The factory had a high accident rate. The complicated machinery of the production line took little account of human error, forgetfulness or ignorance. Day after day, men came out of the factory with squashed fingers, cuts, bruises. Sometimes a man would lose an arm or a leg. Occasionally someone was electrocuted or crushed to death.

'Enlightened people began to see that something needed to be done. First on the scene were the churches. An enterprising minister organized a small first-aid tent outside the factory gate. Soon, with the backing of the Council of Churches, it grew into a properly-built clinic, able to give first-aid to quite serious cases, and to treat minor injuries. The town council became interested, together with local bodies like the Chamber

[2] Quoted by H. F. R. Catherwood, *The Christian in Industrial Society* (IVP, 1964), p. 29.
[3] B. Wren, *A Modern Parable* (published by the Churches' Action for World Development).

of Trade and the Rotary Club. The clinic grew into a small hospital, with modern equipment, an operating theatre, and a full-time staff of doctors and nurses. Several lives were saved. Finally, the factory management, seeing the good that was being done, and wishing to prove itself enlightened, gave the hospital its official backing, with unrestricted access to the factory, a small annual grant, and an ambulance to speed serious cases from workshop to hospital ward.

'But, year by year, as production increased, the accident rate continued to rise. More and more people were hurt or maimed. And, in spite of everything the hospital could do, more and more people died from the injuries they had received. Only then did some people begin to ask if it was enough to treat people's injuries, while leaving untouched the machinery that caused them.'

While taking Brian Wren's point, it is not, of course, by any means accurate to say that the church has shown no interest in promoting social reforms. It was Christians who spearheaded the fight for the abolition of slavery in Britain in the nineteenth century. In defence of the Bible's comparative silence on this particular issue, it could also be pointed out that the harsh realities of political life in New Testament times blocked the outlets for social agitation that are open to Christians now. With few exceptions, the first disciples were men and women drawn from the lower ranks of society. Living under a totalitarian regime, they had no political influence to wield. They could do nothing of a practical nature to rectify the social evils of their day. The seeds of social change were certainly sown in the New Testament's demand for equality between master and slave *in the church* (*cf.* Galatians 3:28), but it would be unfair to reproach these early Christians for failing to take political action.

Working relationships

Nevertheless, such criticisms of Christ and the church do serve to highlight the fact that Jesus' approach to social issues differed in important respects from that of some would-be reformers today. He saw the root of social evil in people rather than in institutions. Being a true radical himself, therefore, his method was to work through individuals into society, rather than vice versa. So, for example, we find him dealing with Zacchaeus, the crooked tax-collector of Jericho, instead of issuing a general manifesto denouncing financial corruption in high places (Luke 19:2ff.). Above all, Jesus sought to bring individual men and women into full personal commitment to God, knowing that genuine faith would have far-reaching social consequences.

Some modern industrial commentators are also stressing the personal factor in dealing with problems of work and economics. For example, Sir Frederick Catherwood, when Director General of the National Economic Development Council, wrote: 'The problems of this age are not technical . . . If you look at the economy of any country and you begin to probe the reasons for slow progress; if you try to find why personal income instead of rising at 10 per cent per annum rises only at 4 or 2 per cent or not at all, then you very quickly discover that the reasons are not technical but human.'[4] The title of the 1971 Industrial *Relations* Act (now repealed) was itself a tacit admission that at the root of industrial conflicts lie bad relationships. Naturally, the improving of working relationships will penetrate to changes in structures. The two inevitably intermesh. But the starting-point is all-important. Should the focus be on organizations and structures – or on relationships and people?

The Bible tells us that one major result of man's fall into sin was the spoiling of working relationships, dating right back to the row between Abel the herdsman and Cain the arable farmer recorded for us in Genesis 4. And the later laws of the Old Testament reflect two areas particularly in which sin ruins relationships – now as then.

1. Seller and buyer

The Bible has some harsh words for tradesmen who cheat their

[4] H. F. R. Catherwood, *The Christian Citizen* (Hodder, 1970), p. 36.

customers: 'You shall not have in your bag two kinds of weights, a large and a small. You shall not have in your house two kinds of measures, a large and a small . . . For all who do such things, all who act dishonestly, are an abomination to the Lord your God' (Deuteronomy 25:13, 14, 16). Micah tells how 'the voice of the Lord cries to the city . . . "Shall I acquit the man with wicked scales and with a bag of deceitful weights?" ' (Micah 6:9, 11).

Although Her Majesty's Inspectors of Weights and Measures have dealt a blow to those who weight their scales and give short measure from their petrol pumps, the cheat is still alive and well in the High Streets of the twentieth century. There are more sophisticated ways today of pulling wool over the consumer's eyes. Misleading guarantees lull the customer into a false sense of security. Inflated 'recommended prices' deceive the housewife into thinking she is getting fantastic bargains when in fact she is only helping to swell already bloated profit margins; and unrealistic delivery dates add to the frustration and disillusionment. If the Old Testament prophets were alive today, they might want to change a few of their illustrations, but their underlying message would still keep its contemporary bite.

More than any other area of business life, one suspects that modern advertising would provide a twentieth-century prophet with a ready-made target. Given an economic system based on competition, some persuasive kind of advertising is inevitable. The producer cannot rest content merely with informing the public of his product's existence. He must do his best to convince those on the other side of the printed page or television screen that his wares are superior to all other brands (even though the 'competing' firms may be members of the same consortium). Inevitably, too, advertisements mirror the standards that already prevail in society. Unpleasant traits in human nature, such as pride, avarice and desire for self-gratification, are harnessed in the seller's interests, and this is a trend that leaves the Christian particularly uneasy. No-one can pretend, of course, that the advertiser actually creates greed, but it is difficult to avoid the conclusion that, in stimulating avarice by the most persuasive means at his disposal, he is strengthening the grip of something the Christian is dedicated to destroy.

It is arguable, too, that the advertiser's tendency to treat the potential customer as a mere unit in profit-making comes very close to the unscrupulous approach to selling which Scripture condemns. Although subliminal advertising is banned by law in the United Kingdom, and it would be an exaggeration to claim that a trip down a London Underground escalator represents the first stage in brain-washing, it is enough to set the alarm bells ringing to discover that some agencies employ professional psychologists to identify and stimulate the consumer's irrational urges. Despite the highly commendable standards demanded by bodies such as the Independent Broadcasting Authority and the Advertising Standards Authority, and the safeguards of the Trade Descriptions Act, modern advertising is still a dangerous weapon in the hands of those with few moral scruples.

2. Employer and employee

As well as spoiling the proper relationship of honesty and trust that should exist between seller and buyer, sin also drives a deep wedge between the worker and those who employ him.

In the power-structures of the biblical world, the boss held all the cards, and Scripture is particularly sharp in condemning employers who used their powers to exploit their labour force. 'Woe to him who builds his house by unrighteousness, and his upper rooms by injustice,' thunders Jeremiah; 'who makes his neighbour serve him for nothing, and does not give him his wages' (Jeremiah 22:13). And in the New Testament we find James sounding the same warning: 'Behold, the wages of the labourers who mowed your fields, which you kept back by fraud, cry out; and the cries of the harvesters have reached the ears of the Lord of hosts' (James 5:4). In face of verses like these, it is curious to find the Marxist still criticizing Christianity as 'the opiate of the masses'.

The sad story of industrial relations in Britain underlines the fact that the selfish, greedy employer has by no means vanished from the modern scene. The drive to maximize profits and improve efficiency means that in some sectors of industry commercial considerations have been allowed to override the human interests of employees, and as Kuyper reminds us, 'to mistreat the workman as "a piece of machinery" is and remains a violation of his human dignity. Even worse, it is a sin going squarely against the sixth commandment, thou shalt not kill.'[5] Ultimately, the gap between humane treatment and efficient productivity may not be nearly so wide as is sometimes imagined. Vehicle producers in France and Italy, for example, are finding that productivity improves once workers are allowed the satisfaction of building a whole car, instead of fixing a single component on a conveyor belt. But there will always be a tendency, especially in the short term, to treat people as tools in the interests of maximum profit, and this is something that has to be strongly resisted on Christian grounds. Very often it is those in middle management who find themselves cast as the villains of the piece. In order not to become victims themselves (and it is no laughing matter to be put out of a job in one's fifties), they feel forced to comply with the constant demands for ever-expanding profit-margins droned out from faraway head offices.

It is here that the trade unions have a particularly important role to fulfil. Much middle-class Christian prejudice against the unions is born out of misunderstanding. The principle of corporate solidarity which arms any group of workers with bargaining power is deeply engrained in Scripture. So, too, is the principle of social justice which the TUC exists to defend. Time and time again in the Bible we are told how God is specially concerned to see that the weak receive just treatment (see, for example, Isaiah 1:17; 58:6ff.; Amos 5:10ff.); and there is little doubt that the individual worker would still find himself both weak and oppressed if he were deprived of his right to associate. The trade union movement also anticipated the welfare state in providing for such things as sickness benefits and funeral grants. It was not for nothing that shop stewards

[5] A. Kuyper, *Christianity and the Class Struggle* (Piet Hein, 1950), p. 57.

29

earned their nickname 'the parsons of industry'.

This is not to pretend, of course, that employers have a monopoly on sin. Employees can be selfish and greedy too. In his parable of the workers in the vineyard, Jesus drew attention to the dog-in-the-manager attitude of those who resent generous treatment offered to others and insist on leap-frogging their wage-rises (Matthew 20:13ff.). He also taught that 'the labourer deserves his wages' (Luke 10:7); but he would not have disagreed with John the Baptist's warning to the professional soldiers who came to him for baptism: 'Rob no one by violence or by false accusation, and be content with your wages' (Luke 3:14). Soldiers in New Testament times were powerful men; they could boost their wage-packets with the aid of threats. Their modern counterparts, perhaps, are those organized bodies of workers who are aware that they control the key areas of industry and are tempted to use their strength to hold others to ransom. A cry for 'fair shares' may be little more than a cloak for greed. In the Old Testament, the principle of corporate solidarity is seen mostly in *national* terms. If this principle were to be applied strictly today, it would presumably mean that employers and employees should sink their differences in working together for the good of the whole body politic.

It is in the light of biblical teaching such as this that the rights and wrongs of *strike action* must be weighed. In 1961, Archbishop Fisher wrote, 'I think it is an unrighteous thing ever to strike for money, except possibly when you are starving.'[6] Many strikes, of course, are not about money at all. But even if we restrict the field to disputes over pay, it is by no means clear that strike action must always be ruled out as immoral on Christian grounds. If an employer is justified in withholding his goods from sale when he feels the price offered is not a fair one, the demands of justice make it difficult to condemn an employee who withholds his labour when he fails to get the proper market value for it. It would be hard to disagree with Joseph Hume's judgment in a parliamentary speech of the last century: 'Labour is the commodity of men,

[6] In a *Daily Herald* article, 26 November 1961.

30

as capital is of the masters, and both are allowed to obtain the best terms they can.'

At the same time, many strikes are blatantly selfish and unjustified. Sometimes they reflect impatience with slow-moving negotiating machinery. The Shop Stewards Handbook of one major union, for example, warns against over-hasty reactions in a time of dispute. All the relevant facts must be collected, weighed and carefully considered before any action is taken.[7] Yet on many occasions men belonging to this union have chosen to take unofficial action rather than go through the set procedures of arbitration. A call for solidarity may mask a very selfish and impatient kind of collective greed. The protests of union officials, that they have no wish to make others suffer through a strike, often have a particularly hollow ring about them.

The Bible upholds the principle of corporate concern, but it condemns the kind of solidarity which has no interest or compassion for those outside the immediate group. Jesus himself told the parable of the Good Samaritan to point out the inadequacy of too narrow a concept of neighbourliness. That is why a just cause will not automatically bring a Christian out on strike. He must first calculate the consequences of his action on others – from the men who will be laid off in a factory fifty miles away, to the underprivileged in other countries who may be paid less for the raw materials they supply – and then weigh these against the size and urgency of his own grievance. In nature, a bird builds its own nest but is not responsible for seeing that all other birds have nests as well. A very similar law of the jungle applies all too often in industrial life, but the Christian cannot be satisfied with anything less than the all-embracing neighbour-love that Jesus demanded.

So much more could be (and has been) written about the causes and cures of industrial problems, but perhaps enough has been said to illustrate the Bible's wisdom in setting its teaching about work firmly in a context of relationships. Working conditions today may be far from ideal. Large groups of

[7] The TGWU Shop Stewards Handbook.

people are employed in vast concerns where personal contact with the employer is out of the question. Directors share their interests over dozens of companies, while many thousands of workers never set eyes on the finished products they are helping to produce. It all seems a far cry from New Testament times. Yet it could be argued with some force that the conditions of work in Paul's day, under a none-too-benevolent system of slavery, were even worse. His instructions to employers and workers at Ephesus and Colossae must have sounded as ludicrously naïve then as they do now. But he and his readers shared something which gave them the potential to revolutionize all working relationships. And that 'something' was their common faith in a God who is himself a worker.

Questions for discussion

1. Do you agree with the statement on p. 23 that the Christian is not entitled to plead 'Give me the right conditions – *then* I will work whole-heartedly'?

2. Should a Christian be prepared to accept lower standards at work than he would in his private life, as an unfortunate but necessary compromise with the need to live in today's world?

3. 'If he finds himself in a minority, the democratic principle demands that a Christian should sink his personal scruples and join in a strike of which he disapproves.' Do you agree?

For further reading
A. Richardson, *The Biblical Doctrine of Work* (SCM, 1963)
H. F. R. Catherwood, *The Christian in Industrial Society* (IVP, 1964)
M. Ivens (ed.), *Industry and Values* (Harrap, 1970)

Part 2: The unpacking

1

'It's all the Lord's work'
Michael Kinch

*Michael Kinch works in the building trade as a bricklayer's labourer.
That means supplying the bricklayers with mortar, cement and bricks,
a tough job physically. David Field concludes that the Bible sees every
man's work as a vocation; but many people would not see anything very
'vocational' in Mike's job. The Old Testament picture of God as a
manual labourer seems to assume the creative skill of a craftsman.
Mike has no opportunity for that sort of work-satisfaction either; but
he does enjoy his work.*

First of all I like working in the open air. I also like the freedom
of not having someone breathing down your neck. You're
more or less your own boss, although, as you work in a gang,
you're responsible to the team. Then there's the building
itself. I like doing something and then seeing the finished
product, then moving on to something else (it might be a
factory or a garage or houses) and when I happen to pass them
again I think, Oh, I built that!

I suppose it can be classed as being boring work; just
supplying bricklayers with mortar and so on. I'm what is
known as a 'nobber', nobbing bricks up the ladder. You put
them on the board and the board on your head and carry them
up. That can be classed as boring, but I get satisfaction out of it.
It keeps me fit, and I find that I can express my emotions
through it and let off steam.

What are you working on at the moment?

We're working on flats in the centre of Derby at the
moment. They're nearly completed. We've been on them
since last August.

Do you like heights?

I don't mind them. I didn't used to like them when I was first in the building trade, but they don't bother me now. I walk along the scaffolding without a care.

David Field points out that not only does the Bible show a working God who is the pattern for all men, but it also sets out a distinctively Christian approach to work. Have you, Mike, felt differently about your work since you became a Christian two years ago?

Yes. I respect authority. I never used to respect authority at all. I used to resent having bosses above me. Now when I'm told to do something I try to do it, to show the Lord in me. That's the main thing, because in the Bible the Lord says we must obey. I find it difficult to work with non-Christians now, although I enjoy the challenge. In the building trade you come up against such a rough bunch; you get blokes who come out of prison and drunkards and tough sort of blokes. They don't respect Christianity, though I'm sure they watch you, and you have to be very careful what you do and say. When I became a Christian I stopped using bad language and so on, though other things changed more slowly. There's still an enormous amount that needs to be changed. I feel the Lord's got lots to do in me.

When you became a Christian, did you question whether you were in the right work?

Yes, Pauline and I felt that the Lord wanted us to work for him. I know we are all working for him wherever we are, in whatever sort of job, but we felt the calling to work for him in full-time service, but we didn't know when. Then we were just waiting. At the moment this is the biggest upset in my job. I've felt definitely since Christmas that I shouldn't be in it, but I've had no definite leading into another job.

Do you think it's wrong for a Christian to be in the sort of job you're in then?

Oh no, of course not. It's a vocation really. It's a calling isn't it, to be wherever the Lord puts us?

How do you know this call?

Well it's peace of mind through prayer, that's how I feel.

36

'A long, dull tunnel that separates Sundays, which are the Lord's days when his work can be done.' That's a quote from David Field on how some Christians view their jobs. What do *you* regard as the Lord's work? Can it be done on week-days just as well as on Sundays?

Well first of all, it's my own job where I am. I feel that the Lord's work is witnessing and living a life to glorify him. I'm working in the centre of Derby and I find it quite easy to give out tracts. I get a varied selection from the church, and try to give them out according to what the person looks like to me, if I have free time. Sometimes you get quite a lot of people coming to you and asking you for them at random. You might get a response, 'What is it?' and I say, 'It's about the Lord Jesus Christ.' Sometimes they reject the tracts. A lot of people have said, 'Thank you' and accepted them. Then I've been on a witness team from my church, helping with services and giving my testimony and so on.

So there's no strict division between the Lord's work and other work.

Oh no! It's all the Lord's work. I just live for him. Some work I'm paid for certainly, but I can't just say, 'No, I'm at work now so I've not got to talk about the Lord.' I can't be like that because my life's given to him wherever I am. If I'm told that I mustn't talk about him, I'd say, 'I'm sorry; I'd rather obey God than you.'

How would you feel the Lord had treated you if you were made redundant?

I'd say, 'Praise the Lord', because I'd just take it as the next step. I know my life is in his hands and he knows all the needs I have for the family and so on.

At the moment you're off work with a bad back. How do you feel about that?

Again I just say, 'Praise the Lord' because I've had difficulty with my job, and I've sometimes felt I shouldn't be there. I've struggled and fought and I've thought, 'I don't want to be here, Lord', and moaned and groaned. I've even started for home feeling ill then felt all right when I got home.

Now you're a Christian do you want a job where you can stretch your mind more?

Well I read a lot now, mostly Christian literature and the Bible. I want to learn as much as possible about the Lord, and background history and the early church. But in my job I can't get any further as a labourer. I've been on a training course for bricklayers; six months, and I could then be considered a semi-skilled bricklayer, but I couldn't find the work. Then, just before I became a Christian, I got a job as a bricklayer's labourer. I'm glad that I can have a job where I don't have to think. I can just praise the Lord and think about things I've been reading. It's good really. Whereas if I had a job where I had to concentrate, perhaps I wouldn't have time to develop as a Christian.

David Field says that much middle-class Christian prejudice against trade unions is born out of misunderstanding, but he sees the principle of corporate solidarity as biblical, and even allows that some strikes are justified. What do you think of the unions?

Well I don't belong to one. There's the Building Trades Union, but I don't think much of unions really. I don't think I believe in the things they go on strike for. If you're in a union, you've got to stick together with the main body, but then if you disagree, you're termed a blackleg, and being a Christian, you couldn't agree with everything they're going to say. There are lots of selfish motives. Before I was a Christian I was money-mad. I used to work hard for money, but now, as long as I get an average wage for what I do, I don't mind. I know the Lord provides and the Lord has provided for us wonderfully.

Can you do overtime in your job if you want to?

No. I do piece-work you see. That's one thing I don't agree with, the ethics of piece-work. When you're on site you get a lot of different gangs building separate houses and there's perhaps one hosepipe between the lot of you and you're fighting for it to fill up the tubs. Everyone wants cement at the same time. As a Christian, I can't think, 'Let them have it' because I'm for my own gang, and we're working for a living. It's very difficult. You have to think of your life as a Christian

and you also have to think of the chaps you're working for.
You're responsible to them as well. You're torn.

Every job has its difficulties for the Christian. Mike says that this work is his vocation because it's where the Lord has put him at the moment. But he's restless and he wants to move. Does your vocation, or calling, change all the time? Should Mike stay in the building trade to be a witness where there are few Christians, or should he stretch his mind in the day as well as in the evening when he devours Christian literature? Should he join a union to make a stand on Christian principles from the inside?

Perhaps the essence of the Christian faith is flexibility; being ready to adapt ourselves to the guidance of God, not once or twice but constantly.

'I'm glad that I can have a job where I don't have to think. I can just praise the Lord and think about things that I've been reading . . . if I had a job where I had to concentrate, perhaps I wouldn't have time to develop as a Christian.'

For further thought:
1. How valid is the point that one can develop better as a Christian in a manual job than in one where concentration is necessary? Is Deuteronomy 6:4–9 relevant?
2. Is it possible to praise the Lord for every eventuality, however inconvenient? What has Philippians 4:10–13 to say on this subject?
3. 'You have to think of your life as a Christian and you also have to think of the chaps you're working for . . . you're torn.' Think of other examples of this kind of problem in other fields. Are there any principles which can be applied?

2

Called to industry
John Kinder

John Kinder is a director of an engineering group

I am responsible for the profitable operation of five factories. My basic job is to foresee problems and to put right areas of loss-making. I endeavour to focus the attention of management on these problem areas. Sometimes I am scolding people and sometimes encouraging them. I think it's a bit like gardening; you need to prune things; you need to put fertilizer on; you need to dig things up; you need to look carefully at what's happening. My objective is to make these companies profitable and keep them profitable.

Where does your work take you?

It takes me to places like the Isle of Anglesey, to an aluminium powder plant, to a foundry in Birmingham, to London, where we make aircraft seating and to Siegen near Frankfurt in Germany where we sell a special type of cast-iron bar.

How did you get started on your career in business in the first place?

I think it goes back to my parents who ran a small business in Leicester. I used to sit doing my homework while they were making out the buying orders. I suppose throughout my time at university I was very interested in industry and business. Then I became an accountant but soon decided I didn't like being in the profession where one was looking at the problems in an academic way and never actually getting involved and trying to solve them. In 1966 I decided to take a job in industry and since then I have enjoyed every minute of it. Although I am

40

an accountant, I have been a salesman, buyer, union negotiator and production controller. I've been involved with the manufacture of chipboard, tanks, pumps and agricultural equipment. I know a lot about quarrying and road-building. For some years I worked for a Merchant Bank.

Were you a Christian when you went into industry?

Yes, certainly. I have been a Christian since the age of 14, that's 25 years ago.

What is your motive for working?

First I do believe that people are fulfilled by working, especially when they're doing something constructive and producing an end-product. As a Christian, from quite early on, I had a bee in my bonnet that Christians tend to look at those in 'holy' professions like school teachers, missionaries, doctors and nurses and think subconsciously that they are somehow 'much better' than people working in industry. These professions are not to be despised of course, but I feel that since the vast majority of people in this country get their living in industry or commerce there should be Christians in those environments who understand the problems and don't look at the thing in too academic a way. I felt very clearly at university, if not before, that God's area for me was industry. I wasn't to go into one of the fashionable professions of evangelical Christians.

In those particular professions, evangelically fashionable or not, they may not have quite so much pressure on them as Christians. It may be that there aren't so many Christians in industry because it's harder to exist there without compromising.

Yes, I think that is true. All I can say is that I feel called to industry and I do find pressures on me as a Christian to compromise. But, at the same time, I have a very clear objective of what I can achieve as a Christian in industry.

And what is that?

I believe that industry exists to create wealth. When I say wealth, I mean jobs for people, houses to put themselves and their children in, products for them to buy; not paper profits; not Rolls-Royces for people to drive around in, but real possessions to enable people to exist and to live happy lives. Where you get bad management, you don't get wealth. You tend to get companies making losses; you tend to get declining industry, unemployment, class bitterness and unfulfilled people. You've got to have a healthy economic basis for society, otherwise all sorts of evils come in. Obviously society consists of sinful people and cannot be purified by 'economic wealth'. However, I believe there is a sense in which there is less cynicism and greater willingness to listen if people are fulfilled by their work and proud of the products they make and of the company to which they belong. I can't prove this. I merely know the effects on people if they work in a badly run company.

Referring back to the question of management, I have found many companies where you can say, 'All right, the management is bad. They were unlucky or they weren't intelligent enough or they weren't qualified enough.' But I would say that in most of the bad cases I've seen, and I've seen some terrible situations, the real heart of the bad management is bad people. Immoral people, people with drink problems, people more concerned with their own selfish ambitions than with the business as a whole. You get one or two people following their own selfish ambitions and the jobs of many, many people can be at stake. So, in a surprising way, I've found that the way to good management is good people. Obviously I have in mind Christian people or people with Christian influences around them.

Do you feel you can serve the community by being good at your job, a good manager?

That's right, although that sounds very wishy-washy when put into the context of the Christian gospel. My work may not be directly for the glory of God as if I were standing up at the roadside, preaching. However, I can take you to several companies in this country where the jobs of three or four hundred people have been saved, not totally, but to a large extent, by decisions made by me. I believe that is to the glory of God.

John, how far has ambition played a part in your career?

Of course ambition does play a part. I have always liked to be

42

in a position where I can do things; get things done myself. I don't have any particular ambition to drive around in a Rolls Royce. I have an ambition to see good healthy companies and, if I can contribute to those companies, that's great. I also have an ambition to see a healthy church and I think that this is another aspect where my experience in industry is helpful. Two reasons; first, I can often help directly, using my business experience in the business side of a church or a Christian organization. But far more important to me is the indirect influence that I can produce, looking at Christian things from the viewpoint of the shop-floor or from one of these back-street engineering companies that I know and like. I believe a lot of what the Christian church says, and the attitudes it portrays, is totally irrelevant to the man on the shop-floor or to the man sitting behind the office desk. I don't know how to make everything relevant but, to be some sort of bridge there, that's an ambition I have.

With such a demanding job, how much time do you have to be involved in your local church?

Not enough. As a family, we worship at our local Church of England church. My wife is fully involved in the young wives group and organizations like that. I'm on the parochial church council and the finance committee. At the moment we're building an extension to our church lounge and I got myself landed with the job of running the fund raising, which is very time-consuming. Occasionally I speak at the local Crusader class. The life I lead contains an awful lot of travel. It does mean that I don't get as much time for direct Christian work as I would like. I am also chairman of the Oxford Kilburn club, which is a home mission activity in North West London. I have been involved with the OK Club for 16 years and incidentally met my wife there. The Christian mission to inner-city areas is another subject close to my heart.

Do you feel it matters if the Christian, who has your sort of job, is not able to contribute in some specific way to a church?

Yes, I do. I view the church as a family and there are some people called to preach and teach; there are other people called to pray. I think people with more time than I have do pray. I know there are people in our church who pray far, far more than we, as a family, do. And I believe there are others who are called to get themselves involved in the affairs of the world and to act as a bridge in that way.

You've mentioned 'called' a few times. Do you really mean to use that word?

Yes. In my career I have taken quite a few tough decisions. I've taken risks in my career. Each time I've come up to an important decision I have felt that the decision I've made isn't from selfish motives; it's merely that I've done what I felt right in the sight of God and that the position I'm in now is basically where the Lord has put me.

Now you mentioned not really having ambition for Rolls Royces, but in your position you must be fairly well off. How do you defend the fairness of it when some people are definitely on the breadline?

It's a difficult question. I wouldn't say that I'm well off. We as a family definitely don't live a lavish life. There are certain areas where, for the sake of the businesses I look after, I have to keep up some appearance of prosperity because my customers and suppliers need to have confidence that my business is not going to go to the wall next week. That is a specific business reason why I don't drive around in a Mini for instance. As for tithing, I endeavour to give a tenth, as we are taught and as I believe is right. You mentioned people on the breadline. . . .

Well, with much poorer salaries than yours. I mean, the difference between £1500 a year and, I don't know, whatever you earn. . . .

Yes. If you are talking about people who sit behind their desks all day, going out to lunch and getting very fat, then I'm with the man on the shop-floor, every day. I would say that if someone examined my timetable and the rackety sort of life I live, they would actually say, 'Yes, it's worth a bit more than £1500 a year.' I would say also that my decisions can influence a lot of other people's lives. I'm very conscious that I have a responsibility there and if I fail then I lose my job. That's the

44

way it works. But if I succeed then I get an above average return. I am very conscious that any power that I may have is only held in trust and the objective is first to serve the Lord and build a society that's honouring to him and secondly, specifically, to make sure one makes profits in the businesses one is involved in.

But your tithe, your tenth, will be bigger than some other people's. Do you feel this is in some way a ministry?

Yes.

It might give you joy to say, 'Because of the situation I'm put in I can give the Lord this money.'

Yes, I think that is right, and when one gives quite a lot of money to a particular society one feels it a challenge to say definitely to oneself, 'I've got to give this; this is a duty, a Christian duty of mine, and I must give.' When one has given, one then feels a lot of joy that one has carried out the Lord's will in this way.

Some people might find in work fulfilment that they don't feel at home; they might be two different people at home and at work. Perhaps you're not the right person to ask this, but do you see yourself as having completely different roles?

I try to be as natural in every situation as I can; being just me. Also, incidentally, I endeavour, or have quite recently endeavoured, to involve my wife with the people that I work with. This is basically because I think that she's a better judge of character than I am and I think that it is right that when I'm away a lot, she should know the people I'm working for and with and she should understand why I'm away.

Some people are embarrassed if their wives come anywhere near their business premises, aren't they?

I'm not, and in times gone by I've taken the whole family round a factory on a Saturday morning. I think they've enjoyed it and I think the work people have as well. I always remember giving the two oldest of our four boys a ride on a fork-lift truck and they loved that.

We often think of businessmen as in the thick of the rat-race. How do you get on in this as a Christian?

Yes, I've met situations which have been very full of politics. Every man is out for his own ends and trying to stab the other man in the back. I've found that, in that type of situation, the business suffers because people spend so much time fighting each other that the basic problems of the business just don't get solved. I always try therefore to get rid of these politics even at some cost to myself. Once or twice I have said, 'Look, I occupy a position here and I don't think I'm the right man; I think there's a better man, like a qualified engineer, rather than myself as an accountant.' I will then say, 'OK, let's put the right man in the right job. Maybe I'll remain as an adviser.' Actions like that tend to create a harmonious team because people suddenly realize that the end, which is to create a good business, is much more important than the individual careers of the people in the business. Therefore they cease to fear that someone else is trying to put one over them; they begin to work more constructively. The business prospers and everyone's careers prosper, which is as it should be.

So it's difficult to know how far to let people step on you really.

I think that if it's in the interests of a business that someone steps on me and tells me, 'John, you're doing no good, you're costing the company money, go away' then I'll go away. But at other times, if I feel that someone is being anti-social within the company and trying to step on me, and he's going to cause problems to the business, then I will fight back just as much as anyone else. My motive will be that I want to see the business and the community, which is within that business, prosper.

Many people feel that they will be tarnished by the world if they go into industry.

Yes, I know. I feel, however, that there are two problems here. There *are* many dishonest businessmen and businesses. I have found that honesty, integrity and openness is possible and indeed is essential to running a good business, so this is not a problem to me. The second problem is that one often has to make decisions that hurt people; like making employees redundant. This is not of course the preserve of industry. A

46

doctor may have to decide between two candidates on a kidney machine. But if this is what is meant by 'becoming tarnished', yes it is part of industry. In these situations I always try to examine my motives minutely before God and I always insist on explaining my decision to the people involved, face to face.

John, thank you.

I hope it is relevant. We haven't spoken much of Jesus and the gospel. That is often the problem of life in industry. However, I hope you have some idea of how this grain of salt is trying to preserve the health of the whole.

'Since the vast majority of people in this country get their living in industry or commerce there should be Christians in those environments who understand the problems.'

For further thought:

1. Since the majority of people in Britain are engaged in industry, should we not assume that most Christians are called to be there with them, unless specifically guided to the contrary?
2. Is 'profitability' a sound guiding principle for a Christian to live by? Does it clash with Matthew 6:25–33?
3. Is giving a tenth of one's income to 'the Lord's work' an appropriate guide for the modern Christian? Are there any differences between life in the time of Leviticus (see Leviticus 27:30–33) and life today? (*e.g.* taxation, 'free will' offering or statutory tithe, giving a proportion of gross or net income, etc). Do they affect the issue?
4. What are our ambitions?

3

'I've never stopped working'
Gillian Wilson-Dickson

Gillian is a housewife. Matthew, aged three, is playing happily and noisily in the kitchen. Oliver is being fed on his mother's lap. In another hour the two girls must be fetched from school, a quarter of an hour's walk away, so there's just time to talk about work! It can't be an undisturbed hour, of course. The telephone rings; the Vicar pops in to check on an evening appointment; Matthew decides he wants his boots on. But Gillian, in the midst of her family, is in her element. You can't easily define work when you're a housewife, nor apportion life neatly into two compartments, work and leisure.

Besides being the mother of four children, who range from four months to six years, Gillian is also the wife of a university lecturer. She is a musician, who gives regular concerts, and she has a talent for writing and illustrating children's stories. To Gillian, money does not play an important role in her work.

I'm not paid for what I would consider my main task. In fact I don't consider work is in *any* sense what I get paid for, because in reality my whole life is my work and my work is my life. I feel that my work is looking after the children, and then looking after the house. My husband earns the money for us to live, and we share it completely. I'm not paid a salary as such. When I go off and give concerts, what most people would call work, I get paid for it; but then I consider that to be my recreation and hobby. It's all topsy-turvy, isn't it? I do consider myself very lucky in the sort of work I do. Not many people can carry on their career while they're bringing up

48

children. Music is one of the few things you can do at the same time as having a family. At the moment I play the viola da gamba, a very old instrument which you wouldn't usually find in an orchestra today, but there's an increasing appreciation of it. In fact before Easter last year I played in ten Passions, St Matthew and St John, and did fifteen or twenty concerts all together between Christmas and the summer.

Gillian gets paid for her recreation but considers her main work to be bringing up the children. But could she consider this her *vocation*?

I feel my main calling at the moment is to look after the children and bring them up. But this doesn't mean that it's going to carry on like that. Obviously it can't. I sometimes wonder if we could foster children later on, but maybe that's just because I feel strongly about bringing up children at the moment; that it is my vocation. I can imagine a time when this will change, but I'm not going to bother too much about that.

People often ask me, 'Have you ever worked?' or say, 'So you haven't really ever worked.' I find this very annoying, and retort, 'I've never really stopped working.' I've always done a bit of teaching and a bit of playing. Some mothers I know have jobs just to give them something to do other than bringing up the children because they get bored or feel shut in. In fact it's very hard to be a good mother if you have nothing else in your life. I think loneliness is one of the main problems for mothers these days. Unless you've got very strong feelings of vocation towards bringing up children it must be very hard to cope with. It's very hard even if you have! A lot of people don't think it's a vocation. They just have children because it's taken for granted that this is what you do when you get married; and also, of course, because of the very strong biological impulse to have children. In the Church of England marriage service, it's the first reason they give for getting married, though not everyone would agree.

Though motherhood is not a 'vocation' for all mothers it is always work. Is the essence of work difficulty and hardship?

4   49

No it isn't. I think it was Shakespeare who said, 'The labour we delight in physics pain.' So although some things are unpleasant, you enjoy them in a perverse sort of way. I mean, it's like labour. David Field talks about labour and work as two different things. I'm not sure that I agree with that entirely. I thought he said that labour is a result of the Fall and work is something in which we copy God. But there can be joy in physical labour.

Of course, being a mother, I tend to think first of the labour of birth. Having a child is terribly hard work and pretty painful for most people. While it lasts you wonder why you do it, then the minute the baby's born it's so fantastic that you wouldn't have missed the experience for worlds! Even the fact of the pain and the hard work has made it more worthwhile. You feel you wouldn't want to be without it. With Oliver it was very slow and fairly peaceful, terribly slow in fact. I had him at home. It was fairly painful, in spite of the fact that I did all the relaxing and things you were supposed to do. I was in labour from about three o'clock in the morning and I had him at about half past eight in the evening. They kept saying, 'Oh this is like a first baby', and telling me stories about women who have their babies in about five minutes! But I had to keep on working, and, of course, I knew the satisfaction of the result of my work.

Yes, work is sometimes to do with results, like doing the garden I suppose. You dig the earth and grub away at those weeds and cut down the dead growth, and plant seeds, and you know there'll be the satisfaction of seeing a clear and growing garden. Then there are other things that are fun in themselves, like changing a baby's nappy. That's work, but not unpleasant to me. It's the same with lots of other activities. We want our children to learn instruments, and we spend some time with them every day, practising and just generally playing around with music. That's a discipline. Some days we enjoy it and some days we don't. Some days I think, 'Oh botheration, we've got to practise. I wish we could just put them to bed,' but on other days it's great fun and very exciting. It's a discipline and a routine, and that's what work is – not necessarily unpleasant, and sometimes with a creative end-product.

David Field points out how man's fall into sin has spoiled working conditions, and this probably has its effect in making our work unpleasant. We are prone to failure in every activity we do and every attitude we take up. I mean, if we were perfect mothers, perfect parents, we'd enjoy being parents much more and we'd experience complete harmony in the family instead of getting on the wrong side of our children. I find that verse, 'Don't drive your children to resentment' helpful. It sums up a lot. I mean, you can drive a baby to resentment by not feeding it when it's crying; you can drive a two-year-old to resentment by insisting on behaviour unsuitable for him; or you can drive a five-year-old to resentment by accusing him rather than helping him to do the right thing. You do all these things because you are not perfect parents. You are carrying out your vocation with sin constantly at hand to gnaw at your pleasure.

I think that the Lord adapts you, as a person, into the right mould at a particular time, for what is your vocation just then. He has helped me as a mother to be very concerned with children. You see when you have just had a baby, or when you're going to have a baby, you are pretty much obsessed by babies, and you can't think about much else. When you've got children you think about children a lot; you talk to friends about the subject; you're working on it, doing research into the subject as you go. You might read books about it or listen to programmes on television about it. I believe God has actually made us like this. Of course this interest wears off as the baby gets older, and you find you are no longer so enthralled by things you thought you'd never get bored by. But then other interests, the next stage in your vocation, take the central place in your life.

Work is a routine, a discipline, a satisfaction, but how can the woman, the mother in particular, interpret the commandment about the seventh day, or as some would call it, the Lord's Day? How can she stop working on a Sunday?

To me, each day is fairly alike. I have days which are kind of highdays and holidays but they're not necessarily going to be Sundays, and they might not be considered to be unworking days by other people. For instance, the last two weekends we've had friends to stay. This has been a great holiday for me, although in some ways it has meant extra work. In other ways it has relieved the load. I didn't have to do all the washing up or bits and pieces with the children that are the normal routine. You see, on a Sunday you can't leave the children in their pyjamas all day. You can't neglect to feed them; you can't not feed the baby on Sunday, though that's not really work anyway. It's very difficult when you're a mother. You can't usually find the time just to sit down quietly and read the Bible or pray. For most children, the quiet or meditating mother is an open invitation to get on her lap. So I tend to be praying as I go.

David Field writes that, 'Vocation extends to all hours as well as to all jobs. The balance between so-called "working" and "non-working" hours may differ between individuals.' Surely that is a tremendous understatement for the woman. In fact David does not really consider the married woman's work load at all. Gillian, as a mother, has to 'work' on Sundays, but so she does for the rest of the week. But what about that category, 'the Lord's work'? In Gill's case it's almost ironic that what can be of direct spiritual help, her Bach concerts, she gets paid for.

I feel that it's a great privilege to play music like Bach, which is specifically on the gospel, and I know, from the people I've talked to, that it can have a very profound spiritual effect on non-Christians. That's very definitely 'the Lord's work'. But normally, when I'm at home with the children, the whole atmosphere of the home, the way I talk all the time, the way I behave, the way my husband and I behave together, the way we bring up the children, those things are far more the Lord's work than anything 'churchy'.

At the moment I don't do much actual church work. At one stage I used to play in the church music group and I did a little bit of visiting and quite a lot of art work when they had a church magazine. And I still do odd bits and pieces like designing a poster or a leaflet, but really not much in the traditional 'church work' line.

To Gillian the whole of life is a varied pattern of different forms of activity, some more tedious, some more exciting than others. Perhaps God's particular gift to each woman is that of adaptability. For Gillian, at least, feeding the baby, playing in concert halls, writing stories, fetching the children from school and entertaining friends, these are all the facets of a richly varied life which is her work.

'*I think that the Lord adapts you, as a person, into the right mould at a particular time, for what is your vocation just then . . . then other interests, the next stage in your vocation, take the central place in your life.*'

For further thought:
1. Is there any point in trying to distinguish between periods of work and leisure? If not, how do we ensure that we get enough leisure or do enough work?
2. What are the principles involved in working, or not working, on the Sabbath? See Exodus 20:8–11 and Luke 14:1–6.
3. Is a vocation for a Christian likely to be for life or must it be reviewed often? Can the principle of Acts 16:6–10 be applied to one's job?

4

'Employer? God, I suppose'
Robin Keeley

Robin is the vicar of a large inner-city church in Leicester, which draws members from all over the city. Robin and his wife and family join most of their congregation by living in the pleasant suburbs a few miles away from the church.

This job involves me in a tremendous variety of work. When I was first thinking towards ordination I had a very clear idea in my mind of what the work of an ordained man was; that it was teaching, both from the pulpit and individually, and very spiritual. But as you can see, my desk is covered with paper. There are other sides to the work as well. One of the things about the ordained ministry and the work of a vicar is that he's really in a leadership role in the congregation. This doesn't only involve his own ministry, exercising his own particular gifts, which are commonly inclined towards teaching, but also involves management. He's in a position where he has to enable the ministry of the whole congregation to be what it should be, and therefore the normal ingredients of management, namely paperwork and sorting out people's problems and holding a whole community in balance, decision-taking and counselling, are all very much part of the work.

Do you have to cope with the administration by yourself?

In my particular case I have secretarial assistance and I don't know how I'd do without it. I know that Parkinson's law says that work tends to expand to fill the amount of time available for its completion, but I honestly don't think that one creates work because one has a secretary. But a degree of administration is an essential in the task. The trouble is that many pastors, if asked what their least favourite job was, would say, 'administration'. Then if they were asked what they spend most time doing they would say, 'administration'. This is the danger, if you are not careful.

Spending time with people is important both in teaching and evangelism, and also perhaps more especially in counselling. So many people today have depth needs, and you need to take a lot of time with them to help them to see Christ's way forward. Mind you, I do have some help in the preaching and spiritual care of the church. In our particular congregation we have a curate and also a clergyman who does a full-time job, but is able to give Sunday help.

When considering a career, how did you decide what you would do?

When I left school I was all set to be a teacher, and I think it was probably during my two years' National Service that I began to see the great need of teaching people what the basics of the Christian faith are. There was a tremendous willingness to hear, but total ignorance of what it was all about, and I think that if that was so in the late fifties it's much more so now.

You could have chosen to teach in a school or lecture in a university.

Yes, that's right; and it's not uncommon for that vocation to move across into a vocation to the ordained ministry. Both are obviously teaching tasks, and if you sense that you are gifted for the one then it's likely that you are gifted for the other. They both involve communication; they both have to do with getting ideas across.

So after National Service, which way did you go?

I was already committed to doing a modern languages degree, and I began to do that. It was during that first year at university that, through the proddings of different people, and through my own thought and prayer, I began to see that ordination was a live option and that I ought to investigate it.

Would you say you were called by God to do it?

Yes, quite definitely. When I talk about the proddings of other people, and what was going on in my own life through my own thought and prayer, I think these are two of the most common ways in which God does call people. They are certainly the way he called me.

How far would you say that every person's work had to be a calling?

I would say it's desirable that every person's work should be a calling, but I wouldn't like to go up to a person doing a job which they would very much rather not be doing, and say they ought to see that job as a vocation from God. I'm lucky enough to be in a job which I find easy to see as a vocation, but I think the *ideal* and the *actual* do rather conflict in some people's sphere of work.

Is it fair, in God's eyes, that some people will enjoy the task of bread-winning, while others hate it?

I really find that question incredibly difficult to answer, because it's a question of how a particular person's life-work appears to them. I mean, how does that question relate to the whole question of unemployment in our own society? I suppose the answer is No, it's not fair; there is a lot of work which people should never be asked to do, but they have no option but to do it. Therefore, in a sense, those of us who have jobs which fulfil us, jobs where we can feel a great sense of God's presence, certainly have a great responsibility to discuss and review the way jobs should be structured as a whole, because work is one of the great ways in which our humanity is meant to be fulfilled.

So you would say that to a certain extent it is sin in society that causes unhappiness at jobs, difficulty in jobs, miserable jobs?

Certainly, yes; I don't think there is any doubt about that. David Field makes the point in his book very aptly that work is a creation ordinance. Mankind is given the work of bringing the creation into proper working order and of mass steward-ship over creation. Then straight after that, in the biblical account, you get the Fall and the injunction to live by the sweat of your brow. I think every job has in it the evidence of both creativity and drudgery. It's the proportions that vary. My job has in it a considerable element of drudgery, although I thought it was all going to be marvellously spiritually creative. I'm sure that every job also has its element of creativity, however repetitive it may be.

How do you assess when you're working and when you're not?

That's very difficult. If you wanted somebody to tell you the truth about this ask my wife! I think that the danger is that you're never not working. I could say I was working from nine o'clock in the morning to ten o'clock at night some days. Yet some of the people I'm working with don't look upon themselves as working. For example, last night I was at the church fellowship meeting. In one sense I was working, because, although I wasn't actually chairing the meeting, I have a leadership role there because of my pastoral responsibility. All those present are working in one sense, and not working in another. But I did look upon myself yesterday as having worked till half past ten. If you are not very careful there is no side of your life which isn't your work, apart from perhaps a day off; and even then your mind is running over some of the problems. You are in danger of thinking of just your job, and just your church, and becoming a real 'church bore'. I think that this is a real danger that 'full-time church workers' are prone to.

Do you have any particular recreational activity?

Well, my recreations tend to be in the realms of reading and sorting out what ideas are coming forward, thrashing them out with friends and so on. That's a bit over-close to my work, so I'm trying to look at other areas, like enjoying the countryside.

You say you sometimes feel you work till half past ten. But in this job you are not paid for the hours you do.

No.

Where does your money come from as a Church of England vicar?

It comes from a variety of places; I won't go into them all, but we can divide them into two. Part of it comes from the Church Commissioners and their stewardship over endowments and investments in the Church of England, and the rest comes from the parish and congregation who give through the diocesan pool. Each parish is giving into a central pool so that richer parishes can aid the work of poorer parishes and so on. My earnings really come from congregations through the diocese and from the Church Commissioners.

Whom do you regard as your employer?

God, I suppose. It's a singularly unsupervised job, which is why some vicars can get away with doing virtually nothing, and others work themselves into the ground. You're not accountable to anybody in particular. I see my bishop, well, I've seen him about twice since I arrived in the diocese four years ago, which is not his fault. There are just too many clergy per bishop. I can feel a sense of guilt or a sense of satisfaction, but it is purely between me and the Lord, and to a certain extent people's expectations. I'm not supervised, and also I'm not really cared for, I think I would honestly say, by anybody in a position of responsibility over me. That would compare adversely with people like social workers, who have the same demands thrust on them, the draining of difficult people all the time, and they have a very careful structure of seniors whereby they can be helped to spill the beans about what is really draining them, and the difficulty of switching off when they go home. I don't get that, or at least I didn't. I think one of the great things is that I have a congregation; that I'm part of a body of Christians now who are beginning to be aware of our mutual problems and with whom I really can feel a sense of common load-sharing.

Some of the money comes from your congregation. They're paying a colleague to care for them spiritually. How do they feel about it?

They don't look upon it like that. I think that's one of the great differences between the Anglican and the Free Church systems. A Free Church congregation, at its worst, can say, 'We pay you to do. . . . ' The Anglican church can't say that because they don't pay the vicar directly.

A lot of your work must be done at home. What are the difficulties there?

Again, you need to ask my wife that question. The difficulties are obvious and my wife and I have looked very carefully into the question of whether it would or would not be better to set up an office at church. In some ways it would, because there are strains with working from within the family. Not only vicars find this, but writers and other self-employed people. The family is around; one of my children is not yet at school and they are both at home in the holidays. There is the danger of just wandering out of the study and then the children feeling that daddy both is and isn't at home. It's a problem. Yet if I were to set up an office at church I would be out in the day as well as most evenings so I'd never feel part of the family. We decided on balance it's better to work from home.

Another difficult area for you is that much of your work takes place on a Sunday, which, for everyone else, is a day when they don't work!

Well, yes, many people think that's the only time I do work! There is an ambivalence here. Obviously my day off is not Sunday. I take another day off in the week, and that's my day of rest, and yet Sunday for the family needs to be a different day. The concept of Sunday, as I understand it, is both a day of relaxation, and also a day of special concentration upon the Lord, and meeting with his people. It's the same ambivalence that comes to somebody who's on shift work, and who has only occasional Sundays off, or a social worker or doctor or somebody, who is on call quite frequently over weekends. It's not unique to the clergy, but it is a problem to be worked at.

We read that Paul was a tent-maker; he did work with his hands. He did a job in the ordinary sense as well as teaching people about Christianity and presumably helping them. How far do you feel it's right just to have spiritual oversight of a church and not be producing anything, either with your hands or with your mind in other ways?

Paul says quite clearly that both are allowable, both are possible. He had chosen a way of earning his own keep so as not to be a charge on the churches in their early days. He also quotes magnificent Old Testament verses like, 'You shall not muzzle an ox when it is treading out the grain', and says that the labourer is worthy of his hire, and that it would be quite allowable in gospel principles for there to be a full-time ministry. Now my view is not that there is too much full-time ministry around but too little. You can have a score of people full-time in our congregation and still find plenty of work for them to do in a society where the vast multitude have turned away from Christ. There is an endless amount of employment for Christians who really are going to be involved in effective ministry. Some churches have found ways of freeing people who are not ordained into full-time ministry, and so I feel no conscience whatever at being full-time. Yet it must be said that the tendency financially is the other way. With the financial crisis that's hitting several of the main denominations, the number of full-time ministers they can afford is diminishing. The Church of England is seeking to beat this by developing a special form of ordination called the Auxiliary Pastoral Ministry where people are employed full-time in their own jobs and yet they are ordained to a full ministry in their leisure time.

They have problems about leisure, don't they?

Yes, and I have my doubts about that personally. It depends what you mean by ordination in my view. How different is that from a lay Christian exercising a full-time ministry within the body of Christ?

Yes, what does ordination do for you?

In my view it does nothing for you that a sense of commissioning by God doesn't do for any Christian. Paul talks about his laying hands on Timothy, and Timothy stirring up the gift that is in him through the laying on of hands. But laying on of hands in the New Testament is for many things, isn't it? for healing, for special commissioning in one way or another. Any Christian, as far as the New Testament is concerned, is a full-time minister. They're in full-time service for Christ, whatever vocation they have to exercise that in. I think that my ordination and my setting apart are more related to the particular role I play in the body of the church, both in the sense that it's a teaching role and therefore I've required special training, and also in terms of its leadership role. As I said earlier I am the enabler, or involved in the enabling of the ministry of the whole body. That is how I understand ordination, but I don't see it as many in the more Catholic end of the church would, in terms of a special embodiment of grace given to me. The priesthood of all believers is something I greatly believe in.

Some people would talk about work, and then 'the Lord's work', and separate them.

I think I was greatly helped by David Field's comment that there was a vocation involved in the whole pattern of our lives; that it isn't just a vocation to work as a teacher or as a minister or as a factory worker and then use the rest of your time to get on with the enjoyable business of working in the church, or the other way round. The whole of the way we live our lives is, or should be, as people called and guided by God.

This question of not knowing whether you're working or not, it's not good for you and it's not good for your ministry because you become less of a person if there is no variety or genuine relaxation or recreation in your life. And so I find I have to make a list of what my responsibilities are over a particular period, cross them off as I do them, and when I've crossed off enough say, 'That's it for now.' I've finished, and I know when I'm going to come back into that schedule, so I can look on myself as genuinely free.

But you're always on call, aren't you?

Yes and no. That's greatly exaggerated. A man has a responsibility to his family and needs to say to any but the most vitally urgent, 'We will fix another time for this.'

'One of the great things is that I have a congregation; that I'm part of a body of Christians now who are beginning to be aware of our mutual problems and with whom I really can feel a sense of common load-sharing.'

For further thought:
1. There are few jobs as unsupervised as that of a vicar in the Church of England. How can congregations be made aware of this problem and how best support their vicar? How far

does the same problem apply in other churches?
2. Is the church a service organization or something more? What are the implications of 1 Corinthians 12?
3. 'The proddings of other people' and 'my own thought and prayer'. Are there any other ways that God uses to guide his people?
4. Is administration 'unspiritual'? See Acts 6:1–4. Note that the men chosen to 'serve tables' had to be full of the Holy Spirit and wisdom.

5

Redundant!
Michael Coupe

Unemployment is high in many parts of the world today. Many students find it difficult to obtain jobs. An alarming number of older people find themselves suddenly redundant with few prospects of alternative employment and less flexibility and energy than their younger counterparts.

How should a Christian approach redundancy or unemployment? In Old and New Testament times there seems to have been little or no problem. There was plenty of work available and not many people needed the highly specialized skills required by industrial society. One could turn one's hand to most things in agriculture or fishing. The man who had no work was merely lazy. Paul had no doubt about it, 'If any one will not work, let him not eat' (2 Thessalonians 3:10).

But in society as it is now organized, a paid job is a privilege and to be out of work is often not the fault of the unemployed but of the system. The church has no right to castigate the jobless as good-for-nothings. Many Christian men and women face unemployment. The books say that work is good and ordained by God. 'I ought to work and I want to work, but I haven't got a job! Have I let God down or has he let me down?'

Can unemployment ever be justified morally? There are some who would justify it economically, but this degrades the working person into an economic pawn. Surely unemployment is not what God wants. Neither is illness. In a fallen world illness and unemployment are inevitable for many. What matters (apart from finding a cure or a job) is how the victim reacts in relation to God. He can become embittered, or he can be wonderfully matured by the experience.

Michael Coupe, a sales manager, has suffered the experience of redundancy more times than most, and when he spoke to Elspeth Stephenson he was by no means sure that his present job would last. Yet he displayed the calm assurance of a man who had never known what it was to be out of work.

Do you believe that everyone has a right to work?

I believe that it is right, in God's sight, for men and women to earn their living. The principle is that God called Adam to till the ground and care for his whole environment. We have a responsibility to care for our families and others around us. There is an infinite variety of ways of working for the common good whether it be productively or as a service or in specialized professions for the spiritual, moral or temporal welfare of the community.

But in a sense, having made Jesus Lord and surrendered everything to him we have no 'rights', only the privileges he gives us. We work to support our own lives and those dependent on us. State aid of various sorts has been provided because it is recognized in an industrial society that some unemployment is inevitable. We are inclined to have 'blinkered' ideas of what work is. We need to remember that God is creative and his ways and means are infinite. As Christians we need to retain the widest interpretation of the word as we see life from his point of view.

What has been the pattern of your working life?

After the War I returned to the family business started years before by my grandfather. For about two years this went on fairly well and then I was made redundant (though it was not called that then) by those in control of the firm. I was out of work from about June to the end of October. Then I started as a trainee with an asbestos firm in November 1948. For the next twenty years I was with them in varying capacities and at the time of leaving in 1969 I had been Sales Promotion and Publicity Manager for the UK and Overseas for seven years. That particular field can be difficult for a Christian as it is all a little 'larger than life'. However I was grateful to have a Group Managing Director who would not allow anything to be published that could not be independently proved. That protected me from having to compromise my principles. I was very thankful for that.

That brings my background up to about ten years ago.

You have been redundant several times, haven't you?

The first time, back in the late 1940s, I have explained. My first real redundancy was basically voluntary. The Company headquarters was moved from London to Scotland and internal changes at the same time convinced my wife and myself that we should not go. Our family was growing up – the elder two were both at university. It would have broken up our family. We had no peace about moving to Scotland. It came home to us that the possibility of redundancy must be faced by all. Christians are not specially insulated from economic exigencies.

Did you have another job in mind to go to?

When eventually I said no, I was prepared to start a small merchant business in conjunction with a friend in Birmingham. That was almost in desperation as I had been to a whole string of unsuccessful interviews. I have realized since that we did not lay this before the Lord first and I believe that was why it did not succeed.

I have been made redundant twice since. First when the firm I was with was sold and the purchaser put in their own management; secondly, at 48 hours' notice, due to an amalgamation of two companies and the consequent redundancy of about 50% of each firm. We were given redundancy money and a month's salary.

Weren't you resentful?

No, I was not resentful, because I had learnt, after the merchant business failed, the meaning of the verse 'Be still and know that I am God' (Psalm 46:10), and to give the Lord his rightful place. As it happened we were due that week-end at a Fountain Trust conference at Swanwick and that time proved a wonderful strength to us. People who had no knowledge of our situation helped us and the Lord spoke to us very clearly in several ways during that week-end. It may sound cocky but we just did not get in a panic. Four weeks later I was offered a job.

How should a Christian approach this problem of being

out of work? What about a school-leaver or a student who can't get a job?

I believe Christians are not exempt from the buffets of everyday life and whatever the problems for a particular generation the principles are the same. I believe, in fact I know, that a Christian will find that Jesus Christ gently, but firmly, insists, that he is Lord completely of our whole lives, in every aspect, every interest, every sphere. You are his and in him and he is yours and in you. He is living his life in you so that you see all things from his point of view. Then whatever the situation may be, no job or never had a job, you have a completely different approach from a non-Christian. You are able to commit the whole situation to the Lord and *be yourself* in him. This does not presuppose that you sit back and do nothing, but it does mean that each step, each interview, is taken knowing that he is living in you. You are walking in his way. I know from experience that when 'I' comes in there is a nudge from the Holy Spirit saying 'aye, aye, you're getting off the path'. I have learnt that the verse 'being in the way, the Lord led me' is true.

You really felt that peace when you had no work?

Yes, because I believe that although there may not be paid work for you there is still plenty that the Lord wants done. There is much you can do with him in the absence of any paid work.

Too many Christians are too much involved in *doing* rather than *being*. I believe we are much more required to *live* Christ, both individually and as a church, and thus our priorities will be right. I believe that there is nothing wrong in accepting unemployment benefit and social security provided by the state. We are certainly enjoined to pay our taxes and to support the government of our country in every way, subject to our consciences.

But what about the family? How did they react when the money wasn't coming in?

Obviously my wife felt that most with housekeeping. We know now that the fellowship we are in would help in real necessity and many acts of kindness have been shown us along

66

the way in each redundancy. Several times money has come without our knowing where it came from. The boys have rallied round. That is all part of the 'body of Christ' working properly, every part contributing to the good of the whole, in things spiritual and in the everyday happenings of life.

You make it sound very easy, almost a holiday. Don't you have to do something about it when you're out of work?

Yes certainly, there are many channels; employment agencies, firms advertising jobs, public appointments, job centres amongst which there will be some jobs that fit your requirements, experience or specialized training. The Lord Jesus went out and mixed with all sorts of people. We deliberately set out to meet certain people. It may be right to contact some friends or acquaintances who may know of possible openings. A life committed to the Lord will make the right decision and know that this is the right job when it comes up. We need to check each possibility with him and learn to ask the right questions so that he can answer precisely, remembering that he can use non-Christians to provide the answers equally well. The whole world is his.

So approach to work is an individual matter. You can't make rules for other people.

Yes. God does not overrule our individuality. He made us and each of us is unique in his sight. He gave us a will of our own to make decisions. A Christian's motivation is the worship and praise and glory of God in all he does and says, in his whole being, to live Christ, in every circumstance, and give full measure to his employer.

'You have a completely different approach from a non-Christian. You are able to commit the whole situation to the Lord and be yourself in him. This does not presuppose that you sit back and do nothing, but it does mean that each step, each interview, is taken knowing that he is living in you.'

For further thought:

1. Does God give a Christian the *right* to paid work? See 1 Corinthians 9:1–18.
2. What is involved in *being yourself*? Honesty? Using your own gifts even if they are not recognized by your church or Christian Union? Facing reality, not an idealized vision of yourself? Who do you think you are?
3. Read Psalm 37:1–7. The advice is easy to take when we are prospering. How can we (a) prepare for the day when we are not prospering? (b) understand its strength when we are out of a job?

6

Just the job for a Christian?
John Marsh

John is a surgeon. He qualified at St Thomas's Hospital in 1948 and is now a consultant surgeon in Warwick. He was honorary editor of The Christian Graduate *from 1961 to 1976.*

I have always thought of a vocation as a job you enjoy doing so much that you accept poor wages. Certainly when I started my surgical career at five pounds a week, all found, it seemed like that.

From a Christian's point of view a surgical career is shielded from a number of problems but runs into others which are not immediately apparent.

In the first place there is always plenty of work to do. It may not always be the sort of work you want because of your training programme. In my generation this was very largely self-imposed. The two examination hurdles on the road to a surgical career after qualifying both had certain job-requirements. Some jobs were known to be excellent for fulfilling the criteria but might not be available at the time you wanted them. It was therefore sometimes necessary to take a job which was less than ideal, for training purposes, in order to provide for the family.

By contrast, some of the good training posts were not ideal for the family, and there were two long years in which I only came home every other week-end.

Nowadays there are far more planned training schemes which avoid these difficulties. Now I have climbed the training ladder to my present post of consultant surgeon there is little likelihood of unemployment. New cures are always being put forward which will supposedly do away with the need for the surgeon, but, even if the motor car, which can bring in eleven or so cases to my hospital every week-end, is abolished, there seems little chance of the flow of work drying up.

Faced by the waiting list of things to be done I sometimes feel as though I am under a waterfall. However much water rushes away from me, allowing me to breathe, there is always another torrent about to fall on my head.

The work is never boring. I teach my juniors the need to be able to change gear. There may be times when life seems a little routine as though you were cruising in overdrive on some empty motorway, but the tempo very quickly changes and you must be prepared to deal with it. Suddenly the scene alters; there are bends with unknown hazards and the road is now more like a hair-raising hill climb. In the days when I read motoring journals about hill-climbs like that there was a phrase about 100% motoring, and that is what it can be like. Suddenly the situation demands everything you have got. For example, what may have started as a routine operation suddenly reveals an abnormality that no-one could have foreseen. If the surgeon was concentrating before, his vigilance is now re-doubled. If his assistants know him they will know that this is not the time to come in with telephone messages.

Or again, a routine day may be suddenly transformed into a late supper day by a pile-up on the by-pass. Surgery can be ulcer-provoking at times, even hair-raising, but never boring.

Fortunately the stress does not go on indefinitely, otherwise no-one would stand it. In the war it was shown that after eight hours' operating, the surgeon's efficiency fell off and longer hours became non-productive. There has to be a period of unwinding. I have now got to the age when this includes a snooze in the chair after supper on a long operating day. Of course, the need to unwind is the basis of all the *Doctor in the House* stories and *MASH* films.

A further result of the acute work-load is that the surgeon learns to make decisions. Hornblower says somewhere, 'Better a bad commander-in-chief than a divided command.' In the middle of the night there may be no perfect answer to some surgical problem. What is certain is that if you wait to get a committee decision the patient will be dead.

This stretching of the faculties under demanding circumstances continues to the end of one's career. There is always something new to learn, something no-one has so far foreseen. As Hippocrates said, 'The art is long and life is short.'

Working relations

For all I know my working patterns are mirrored by other jobs, but they seem unusual enough to warrant some discussion.

First, with regard to my employer, I am in a privileged position. I work for the National Health Service who pay my salary and provide me with the environment within which I work. When I was appointed I underwent a statutory selection procedure which was only the end of a long and rigorous training; in itself a selection procedure. Having thus appointed me the NHS does not wish me to go. Indeed, although I have never put the matter to the test, I understand they would make it difficult for me to retire before a suitably advanced age. But whilst in the post, I am given a very considerable measure of trust by my employer.

Thus, if I admit a patient for surgery, I am involving the country in expense. According to the type and degree it may be a considerable expense. I am a general surgeon involved in children's surgery for about a third of my time and as such am not in an expensive class such as open-heart surgery. Even so the costs are considerable. As I quote figures I am aware that the situation will have been taken upwards even by tomorrow. A bed in a ward costs £100 a week to maintain. A bottle of blood is £30. An operating table (which lasts up to twenty years) costs as much as a Mini. But although all this plant is expensive, about 70% of the NHS costs are wages.

When I initiate a patient's admission to hospital for an operation it is not only my own salary that is involved. There are

71

nurses to nurse and make beds with linen that has been laundered in a hospital laundry (maintained by engineers), delivered by porters, paid for by treasurers. Then blood samples are taken by technicians, analysed in a laboratory that stores its data in a computer. There are X-rays to be taken by radiographers, muscles to be exercised by physiotherapists, diets to be prepared and cooked, social workers to sort out home problems and so a whole interlocking series of expensive services are called into play. Some result from emergency admission but many from admissions I have initiated from out-patient attendances.

The resident staff, the ward sister, the physiotherapist, the social worker and I go round the ward together twice a week to see each patient in bed and to sort out problems and decide policy, a very valuable mobile committee. The ultimate decision after consultation is, however, mine. That is to say I am the person who will be sued if things go wrong.

There are obviously many ethical problems at this stage. It will be the consultant who takes the responsibility of telling unpleasant truths to patient and relatives. This is usually best done by coming back at some quiet time to have an individual discussion.

As a job involving government money immediately there must be questions of cost effectiveness and accountability. The latest TV medical series seems to be all about this.

As a result of its origin in Christian compassion the medical profession has never been very interested in cost effectiveness. We do expensive operations to make old ladies living in geriatric wards comfortable. We spend long hours patching up psychopaths who have crashed cars so that they can go out and steal another one and do it again. Lord Rutherford said, 'There is no money, gentlemen. We must use our brains.' If there is not much cash the surgeon thinks of ways to improve his efficiency before the administrators do. Short-stay wards, day visits, and many other devices have been explored to improve the number of operations per unit money.

It still does not solve the problem of who has priority on a waiting list. The hernia sufferer working on an export order or the schoolmaster with an ulcer? In my area we seek to do farmers during their slack season, which is about a month a year, but the other decisions are a constant juggling of facilities, needs, and expertise available at that moment.

When our political masters decide that abortions and sterilizations are to be provided under the NHS they leave to us, or rather my gynaecological colleagues who are already stretched with curative surgery, the decision where and when to deal with this extra load.

All this has led to the concept of medical audit when we meet with our colleagues and analyse our cases and results to decide how effective we are and whether we should modify our methods.

So far the responsibility remains in our court and it concerns all doctors. Christians and non-Christians alike exercise our freedom of clinical judgment within the bounds of an ethic which, implicitly or explicity, is based on Christian principles.

Relationship with juniors

My relationship with my juniors (that is, members of my surgical team) is also interesting and non-hierarchical. I have a large say in the appointment of junior staff, a responsibility shared with my colleagues, but their contract is with the local health authority. I have no control and little influence over their terms and conditions of service. I can ensure, or try to ensure, that their problems about pay, leave and accommodation get through to the right quarters, but I have no authority to alter them. I control the team in the sense that I plan the work load and allocate each task to the person best fitted to it, houseman or registrar. But I am also the chief technician in the sense that if the problem is a difficult one I have to deal with it myself.

I show my juniors how to do things and they do their share of the work. Most important of all I try to teach them to recognize the problem that is going to develop into something for which they need help. They are in the front line now, but they need to know the danger signals that lead to my being called into the front line. To begin with, this is not easy. When a registrar is new I am called from my bed more often than when he is more experienced. Then I have to start the cycle all over again. But when the going is tough with a bad emergency, it is the consultant who has to come in to deal with it. Middle-of-the-night work gets tougher as you get older, and there is no time off in lieu the next day.

My relationship with my juniors is thus like an old-fashioned apprentice system. They come because they want to be taught and I choose them because they have potential to be taught. There is no greater reward than seeing them going on to be fully-fledged surgeons in their own right doing some things better than I can.

Hospital doctors begin, after qualifying, as house officers and stay only six months. I now have a formidable list of those who have worked with me. It is only with a proportion of these that I am in touch, though I know where most of them are.

The registrar grade however is a longer job. Most stay one to two years, during which time we coach them through their higher degree. Over this time a close working relationship develops. They then leave for the next rung on the ladder. At first you know exactly what they are doing because they want references. My first four registrars are all in consultant posts now and remain good friends.

Some among the junior staff have been Christians. In some instances we have not found this out about each other until the interview. If a student has been on his elective period to a mission hospital you soon find a common interest. If your juniors attend the same church there is a closer relationship developed.

Politics

We cannot leave working relationships without considering political action. Most surgeons and doctors are not by nature political animals. Those doctors, and they are few, who become successful politicians have usually given up practice.

74

There are many more ex-doctors in literature, from Keats to Somerset Maugham, than there are in politics. My father used to say, 'Show me a hundred doctors and I will show you a hundred blacklegs.' In the nature of an individualistic profession there is an aversion to united political action, but this is changing before our eyes in this generation. Doctors' pay was under a gentleman's agreement for many years. Today there is a general feeling that now there are no gentlemen but lots of bills, there has to be some rethinking. Those Christians who have sat on negotiating committees have found it tough and unpleasant, but this is another subject in itself.

The Christian surgeon

In all this I have made the assumption that surgery is just the job for a Christian. And indeed this is so in popular esteem. It is near the top of the list of 'acceptable jobs for Christians', described by David Field. It all seems to be splendidly OK. We are involved in a ministry of healing; we are concerned in people's lives. We are allowed to be late for church meetings. We can miss worship on Sundays and everyone thinks that is fine. But there are problems too. What are we really meant to be doing? First we have to ask whether compassion is a sufficient motive. It is plain that patching someone up after a road accident comes into this category. But what happens when we move to plastic surgery that is merely removing an ugly scar; or to an operation that helps someone to walk a bit further than they otherwise could? Are there any limits that can be set to our task? How far are we entitled to think that we are helping to restore man's body to what God originally intended? Or is the Christian surgeon's work merely a means to an end to allow him to speak to his patients of the more important spiritual matters? This is an unspoken question from friends in the church just as it is spoken openly to Christian social workers. It is very relevant to the missionary surgeon.

Recently I received a prayer letter from a young doctor

75

friend in Niger which said, 'I think, at present, we have lost sight of our true *raison d'être*. We should be primarily proclaiming the Good News of Jesus Christ. The medical work of the hospital is secondary to this, the means by which the people are drawn together to hear the gospel. But with so many problems and ever increasing demands for physical healing, the medical work becomes a big time and energy consuming end in itself and our priorities turn upside down, I'm sure much to Satan's relief.'

The problem is acute for the missionary doctor but has to be sorted out by every Christian doctor. For my part I believe I am called to be as good a doctor as possible and not to be an evangelist. I was much influenced in my youth by the bad impression given at a certain hospital by a Christian who was never available for emergency surgery because he was always preaching. Experience therefore influenced me first, but I believe it is confirmed by the scriptural doctrine of work that we are called to be witnesses first by the quality of our work. How may this be done?

A common problem for discussion at a meeting of Christian doctors is how to shine when our non-Christian colleagues are clever, hard working and compassionate. Some of them, indeed, are more clever and possibly more hard working than we are. My experience is that it is becoming a little easier for the new generation of Christian doctors as the inherited Christian ethic which has so influenced medical practice wears thinner and thinner. Certainly I have had it said to me of one of my Christian juniors, 'Dr X is what I call a real old-fashioned doctor.'

Now if some of our friends at church are unhappy that we are not using our positions to evangelize, some others have a feeling, which seems more prevalent these days, that medicine is different from healing. As they might put it, 'Medicine is all very well but healing is spiritual. When the doctors fail then oil and prayer may work.'

I personally think this view denies God's power over all his creation. He is upholding the universe by the word of his power. In Spurgeon's words, he did not wind up the world like a watch and then put it under his pillow. All healing is his gift. When I suture skin or internal organs, when I splint broken bones, they heal because of the properties with which God has endowed them. Studies in wound healing are searching out the wonders of God's mechanisms. Over the entrance to the Cavendish Laboratory in Cambridge are still, I presume, the words, 'Great are the works of the Lord and sought out by all those who have pleasure therein'. As it is with physical research, so it is with medical. The moulds that provide the antibiotics are God-given, as was the skill of the bacteriologist and chemist that isolated and synthesized them. Prayer is not an extra to be added as the final tincture in a prescription whose other ingredients are neutral or even devilish.

All healing is from God and I consider such skills as I have a gift from him. Were Luke's gifts included among the charismata? I think Paul availed himself of them. I think doctors can consider themselves among the healers the New Testament mentions.

The 'Lord's work'

But even if the surgeon's work is useful and God-given in itself, he will almost certainly want to use his talents in the church fellowship as well. If he is on duty a lot he may find it difficult to have a regular commitment to a Bible Class, although the men's class at Bristol, run for many years first by Professor Rendle Short and then by Dr Bill Capper, shows that even this is possible. I am personally grateful that I was able to edit *The Christian Graduate*, which I could do from home, and at antisocial hours which fitted in with times on call.

Wherever they are, doctors have to be used to the familiar words, 'I know I should not bother you at church but could you just tell me how so and so is? Do you think acupuncture would help my uncle? Which is the best doctor to change to?' Living in a small town, and having recently been shown an abdominal scar in Boots by a grateful patient, I am fairly immune to this. I understand it is just as bad for lawyers (except

77

for the scar problem). But it makes it very difficult for medical men who are only just enquiring about Christianity to come to church, and I now understand why my father would drive twenty miles to the peace of Manchester Cathedral.

So although I have sometimes exclaimed in the middle of the night, 'Why did I take this job?' it has never been said seriously. I would not change for the world, despite falling status, frozen salaries, lack of facilities, bureaucracy and the rest. I enjoy it all very much.

Despite all the separation from wife and children when I was training and all the complications of arranging to go out together now, I do not think they want me to change either.

'I believe I am called to be as good a doctor as possible and not to be an evangelist . . . I believe it is confirmed by the scriptural doctrine of work that we are called to be witnesses first by the quality of our work.'

For further thought:
1. Is medical work an excuse to preach the gospel?
   (a) At home.
   (b) On the 'mission field'.
   See Ephesians 6:6, 7.
2. How does a Christian's quality of work differ from that of a dedicated non-Christian colleague? Colossians 3:23, 24.
   Should we be pleased that even a non-Christian's life is admirable, or annoyed that our example is not able to be much better than his?
3. It is possible to overwork. What principles should be applied to prevent it? Mark 6:30–32.
4. Is it possible or useful to distinguish between medical cure, 'natural' healing and miraculous healing?

7

Nothing comes automatically
Elspeth Stephenson

Elspeth is a free-lance broadcaster working mainly in local radio.

Being self-employed means paying £2.20 per week for national insurance, or at least letting it slip conveniently out of a bank, and always working to earn money. Nothing comes automatically. You can't sit down in a cosy groove and let events take their course. You have to make them move. For the Christian there is the prime assurance of the Divine Mover, who is working out his pattern in those events and with you, but this doesn't mean you can sit on your backside and let the world flow around you.

Looking back at my succession of jobs, I find that I've worked in different but connected fields. I don't like the word 'career'. It seems to me to embody a self-centred drive to the top, which isn't always what the Christian is required to do. After university, I worked for several years as a children's librarian, serving youngsters, matching them with the books, and needing to know the person and the page intimately. Then I worked as a children's book editor with a Christian publisher. Once more I turned to librarianship, but in the local history field, and I've also worked in the home office of an international missionary society, editing their magazine.

At each stage I've known that it's been right to move to the next. It's been clearly marked each time. Now I find myself in the position of having 'edged into' local radio. I say 'edged in' because I started as a voluntary contributor to a Christian programme and, little by little, was given more paid jobs. I realize that my voice is suitable for radio work, and this, happily, is nothing to boast about, because you don't 'make' your own voice (apologies to any Eliza Doolittle who may be reading this!).

This leads on to a very important point about free-lance work. You are paid for each item of work you do, however long it takes you. I think to myself on these lines, 'If I can do a good interview on that celebrity in town, and it's accepted, that will be another five pounds and I can buy that blouse I need.' The money doesn't come easily. You have to work for it, but there is a tremendous God-given satisfaction in being paid for a job well done. Yes, I can appreciate the indignation of some of you who earn salaries, who work hard throughout the day, but there must be times when you can ease off, when the work doesn't come in and you sit there bored at the office desk. You still earn your salary. I have to face the fact that if I don't work, I don't get paid. Likewise if I'm ill I don't get paid. I'm learning not to get uptight about this. After all, the Lord has given me good health, and he is in over-all charge. Mine might look a precarious career, but above any boss who might give or withhold work here, I am certain that there's one who's planning my life in the way he wants.

In some posts I have been unhappy, and I've known this was for a purpose. I'm glad to say that my present work is really interesting. It may be frustrating, nerve-shattering, tiring, but it is never dull. Besides producing the children's programme at the moment I go out and about doing interviews, and I really enjoy meeting people and establishing a relationship, even though of necessity it has to be a temporary one. There are people who are rude from the start, they lay at your door any complaint at all against the whole of the media (perhaps some announcer gave a wrong football result or we don't play enough pop), but most people respond very happily. The variety is enormous. One day I might be interviewing a ninety-one-year-old who's spent thirty years in the fire service. The next day I might be learning to fly a very small aircraft, and then talking to a child who is bottle-feeding a new-born lamb. Each interview is a challenge and a fresh encounter with another life.

That's the 'people' side which I enjoy. Then there's the ideas side. I thought I was an 'ideas-person' until I had to think up workable ideas in a very short time! The children's programme, in particular, is a happy field for my inventive imagination. I enjoy creating a feature, editing the tape, juxtaposing different views, writing script that's readable, lively and informative. It's good!

I must say also that I enjoy the immediacy of the work. If you write a book you may have to wait a year before it is published. If you work for radio, an afternoon announcer will be advertising your feature on, say, arthritis, for the following morning, even before you've gone out and obtained the interview! Such work compares favourably, for me, with the endless delays, committees, copies in triplicate and hierarchies of decision makers who can deaden and stifle ideas in some large organizations. Working in the media, particularly in local radio, where the small budget is stretched thin, does show what can be done by a few people in a very short time. Pressure concentrates one's energies wonderfully. An instance of this was when I realized I had no serial story lined up for the next few weeks in the children's programme. We can't use printed material, as copyright fees are too high, so we have to find local unpublished work. I had been let down by a couple of sources, and by that Tuesday knew I had no story to record on Thursday of the same week. So I just had to sit down and write a serial story then and there. I managed it, six episodes in two days, because I *had* to. It was rather a hack job, but it served. This makes me observe that Christians in management should constantly be looking at which jobs are necessary and where too much time is being spent.

There are the usual frustrations that I suppose you get in every job. You might phone around all morning and get only negative responses when you need to set up three interviews that day. You might start to edit a tape on one machine only to find that a news producer has an urgent phone-call coming through from, say, Beirut, and needs the studio, and then when you find another machine, the cleaner needs to come in.

But I expect everyone could give similar examples. A phrase I heard once sticks in my mind. 'Turn set-backs into spring-boards. It isn't what you *do*, it's what you *are* that counts before God.' Then as a free-lance who can't get on with her work, I don't find it easy.

Again, there's the difficulty of fighting for work and pay and yet retaining the clothing of humility we have as Christians. Personally I hate fighting for anything, but often I have to negotiate a fee. Where do you draw the line in being willing to be trampled on? When do you fight for justice? Do you allow yourself to be exploited? You may be quite prepared to find your personal tea-bags snaffled for the dire need of a thirsty colleague, but not so happy about the studio you've booked being taken over just because you are the person with least rights in the whole set-up! I think part of the answer must be a soaking in the Lord Jesus Christ, in his Spirit, in his Person and power, so that you are able to do the right thing by him in each particular instance.

Although I have left behind the half-hour Christian programme which I used to compile and present each week, and have moved more into 'secular' radio, do I serve the Lord any the less? I am not able to broadcast the good news of Jesus Christ very often over the air, but because Christ is in me, there must be some tang of wholesomeness coming across.

Of course there are difficulties. When you are presenting a programme on the air, linking taped interviews and music, you may not be in charge of what subjects are treated or how they are dealt with. I have found, however, that compromise situations are few. It's as well to listen to records all through, though, and you just have to set your standards to the level that your close relationship with Christ demands. Throughout, it's good to have the loving prayer of a caring church fellowship.

At one time I used to help in a church group for 10-14's held in my home; Sunday mornings and an evening in the week. I also used to do a few other jobs within the fellowship. But working with radio, I found for the first time that my paid work took nearly all my energies, and that I couldn't plan a week. You can't arrange all interviews between 9 and 5 Monday to Friday. I went through a real tussle with the Lord over the rights and wrongs of leaving specific church work to others. I wanted, and want, to be a functioning member of the body of Christ, not only living him out but giving time to service. I felt guilty at first, when I decided that I couldn't manage church work. But I explained, and people understand. Now I am getting back to 'one-off' helping, for instance, at an outreach service now and again.

I think that the church, the local body of believers, could really minister to each member in praying for each other's secular employment. Do you know the secular occupation of all the members of your church? Does what they do in the day concern you? You may share your own spiritual needs, but are you free enough to share your work problems? I am fortunate indeed in that my fellowship has 'taken me on' in prayer. I am their voice on the radio and they pray me through difficult times. We are whole people, and if our work is God-given, a vocation, shouldn't it be of primary concern for us to pray for each other? If work is not to be the 'dark tunnel' that David Field pictures, it must be shared with the fellowship of believers, the church, and prayed through. Because I have no specific church job I can't often be sharing news of it at prayer meetings, for my field of witness, which is putting it much too grandly, is just where I work.

I find that the times when the church meets for worship, prayer or Bible study, become more precious because now I can't always be there, due to work commitments. If one were not committed to Christ, it would be easy enough gradually to edge out of the deep fellowship of the church. It has to be understood, too, that some Sunday work is inevitable, particularly if you are working on a Christian programme. You need to interview speakers at services, or produce some listening for Sunday itself. Then I think that if Christians accept that there should be radio and television at the week-ends, they should accept the need for Christians to work on Sunday. As a free-lance, however, I do have some choice in the work I accept, and now I try to keep Sunday completely free.

It's still not easy to say exactly when you are working or when you are not working, and also to discipline yourself to stop. As a free-lance, you know that if you work a bit harder you may get a bit more money, so you have to insist on leisure. At a certain period, some months back, I found myself completely exhausted, and looking in detail at my pattern of life, I found I was working every morning, afternoon and evening except Sundays. You have to limit the time you work, even though you enjoy it a lot. Sundays I try to keep free and then I sleep, eat, worship, relax with friends or in the garden or with books.

I must mention one misconception that people have, that a single person is *free*. Indeed, I don't have children to tie me down, and keep me house-bound, but I have to earn my daily bread, and cook it, and look after my accommodation and garden. Most people would agree that work is a satisfying and useful way of spending time, that it's a service and it gives them money to live on. But for the single girl (except the landed rich), unlike her married sisters, she just *has* to work.

As to whether my present work is to be called my vocation, I would say an unqualified yes. But what about some years in past jobs, when I've been utterly bored and clock-watching? I know for a certainty that I was in the centre of the Lord's will, even then, because in every move I made I was assured that it was the right step. Maybe we should leave this word 'vocation' out of our vocabulary, and just aim to follow the Lord's directions daily, and let that be sufficient.

'... one misconception that people have, that a single person is free ... but I have to earn my daily bread, and cook it, and look after my accommodation and garden ... but ... in every move I made I was assured that it was the right step.'

For further thought:
1. In practice how do we divide our thinking between 'making things happen' and letting God take over? Consider

examples such as applying for promotion or waiting to be noticed. Does it depend on one's personality?

2. Free-lance work is exciting and challenging. Would it be responsible for a married man with a family to follow such an 'insecure' calling? With Matthew 6:25–34 consider 1 Corinthians 7:32–35.

3. How far should a Christian fight for his rights? Or should he be a doormat for the world to wipe its feet on? Ephesians 6:1–20 suggests both humility and strength. How do these qualities match up in practice? Think of examples.

8

'Teach? Definitely not!'
Mary Hemes

Rowlatts Hill really is a hill! A spiralling road climbs the steep ascent and encircles the newly-built estate. Crowning the hill are several skyscrapers and on the 22nd floor of one of them lives Mary Hemes, a school teacher. It was pleasant to step out of the impersonal lift into a tastefully arranged flat, with a view that many would envy. The view no longer takes Mary's breath away, though she notices changes in the landscape. More 'little boxes made of ticky-tacky' gradually push the green spread further away.

Every day Mary descends from her ivory tower and travels to school where she teaches Latin to girls aged 12 to 18, a subject some might consider as much 'up in the sky' as her flat. She's been doing this for thirteen years now, and her vocation to teaching was certain.

I decided I wanted to teach when I went to an Inter-School Christian Fellowship conference, when I was in my last year at school. I had no idea what I wanted to do except that I *didn't* want to teach. Definitely not! But there was such a good speaker who explained how you might help yourself and others by teaching, that I really thought about it again. As a Christian I knew I could serve the Lord in this way. And I've certainly found that this is so. It wasn't my idea. I didn't like the idea of standing up in front of a class, I couldn't do it in my own strength, let's put it that way.

When people pray for guidance about a career they often have a dark fear in the back of their minds that the thing they least want to do must be God's will. The sacrifice of their desires, even their gifts, seems to them to be appropriate. Usually they come to see that God calls both

86

to want as well as to do his good pleasure, as Paul has it in Philippians 2:13. But is hating the idea of a calling a sufficient reason for abandoning it?

I went to the ISCF Conference in my last year at school, where the emphasis was on vocation and allowing the Lord to use you where he wanted you. The need for Christian teachers was stressed among other things, the opportunities for service in that field being unique. This was where the Lord made me realize that this could be what he wanted me to do and although I still hated the idea, relying on my own strength, I realized that he could over-rule and use me in this way.

Gradually, with his help, I got through the throes of teaching practice and on to teaching itself. In my own strength I still have no liking for the position as such, but with the Lord's help, I can overcome and can utilize the opportunities.

I think there is much to be said for having to trust in the Lord completely in order to do one's job. In my opinion, in many ways it is much more valuable than to be doing a job which you like and have no problems with, because there is the possible danger then of self-reliance.

Obviously God can call us to do different things in different ways. He knows best, but it is wonderful to think of your job as well as your life as a partnership when you become a Christian.

Of course, to Mary, as to most single people, a job is necessary to earn enough money to live reasonably, but it is also necessary for fulfilment. Even the 'idle rich' want the satisfaction of a job. In the light of David Field's supposed 'spiritual league table' of approved Christian jobs, Mary Hemes is secure. To be a teacher almost *implies* the old meaning of vocation. Now Mary said she could 'serve the Lord' by teaching, but what does this actually mean in practice?

I think the main way is not so much in teaching but in the pastoral side of the job. You have a form for two years at a time. You get to know them. You can help them out in all their problems. You can point them in the right direction un-obtrusively, and if you are not connected with religious education or religious knowledge lessons you have a specific advantage. The girls have no fears that you're 'getting at them', and, of course, you're not.

Even in a school with Christian standards there are problems.

In the staff-room there are considerable difficulties, where there are only one or two Christians on the staff. You tend to be ganged-up-against, regardless of whether the staff know or care what you stand for. Then there are problems among the girls. If they find out you're connected with the Christian Union for instance, they tend to clam up, which encourages me to have less connection with the CU. I feel I can do more good by approaching them in a slightly different way. The girls need to be able to *trust* you.

Now Latin isn't one of the most controversial subjects, but Mary told me of the occasional dilemma!

There are problems about paganism. A parent wrote to the school recently, complaining that her daughter had been writing a curse for homework! She thought that this was not really suitable for a school with Christian standards. So we had to explain that the girls were only doing an exercise. They had been discovering how curses were found in ancient Britain, written backwards, and were invited to try the same sort of thing, really as a game. But it back-fired some-what, and I found myself justifying my actions in front of the Head.

Besides school work, Mary has her flat to look after. She's actively involved in the Scripture Union committee in the city, and with Scripture Union holiday missions, so she doesn't have much time left to be heavily commit-ted to her local church. I wondered how far she thought a Christian should put a lot of time and effort into 'Christian' work outside everyday work.

I think that's part of God's plan for the Christian. But you can't put *everything* into your everyday work and *everything* into Christian activities outside your work. It's got to be a balance,

I would think. If their own work leaves people too exhausted to do outside Christian work they might need to re-think, and ask the Lord's guidance about it. Not only do they lack energy for the Lord's work but they may be too exhausted to go on with the Lord at all. I don't see 'the Lord's work' as *more* important than my teaching. It has to be about an equal balance. If you think about your work as a vocation, then it's just as important as the 'Lord's work' in inverted commas.

There is pressure of work from all angles, a familiar problem to many Christians who do a lot of voluntary work. What is the secret?

You've just got to organize yourself to make use of all the time available for teaching, part-time Christian work, housework. If I weren't organized I'd *have* to become so, in order to get everything in. God wants us to be organized to bring glory to him.

Organization is an underestimated gift of God, but it has been given to Mary Hemes. She also has a rare gift of honesty. Few would admit to being called to something they don't enjoy thoroughly, yet it must be admitted that most Christians find their work hard, sometimes tedious even frustrating. Mary may have given the impression that she is a highly-organized martyr. Does she really appear to be like that?

The best judge of a teacher is probably a pupil. What impression does Mary give to the children she teaches?

Gill, aged 13, writes:
I have quite liked Mrs Hemes[1] from the time I first met her. She seemed a bit strict but she had a good sense of humour and was making us laugh before very long. She's a very good teacher. When she's in a good mood the lessons are really great because she keeps making us laugh by making comments about the pictures in the pamphlets and reading from the Teachers' Handbook.

[1] Since this interview was recorded, Mary has left her skyscraper flat and is now married. Her married name is used throughout.

There are certain people in the form that she is always making comments about. I'm one of them. I suppose it is because I've got a similar sense of humour to hers. She makes comments, so I make comments back. My mum always tells friends that the Latin lessons include only two people, Mrs Hemes and me. However, I don't think that's quite correct. Despite all the comments we *do* get quite a bit of work done.

When she's not in a good mood though the lessons aren't so good. She is very strict then and we do considerably more work (not that that's a sin!) but she doesn't even smile, let alone make comments.

You can usually tell what mood she's in when she comes into the form-room. She's usually in a bad mood on Thursdays! I suppose it's because she's tired on Thursdays. It follows, as she's usually in her best mood on Mondays.

Near the end of term she's nearly *always* in a good mood which is better.

She is friendly and she has a pleasant personality and she's one of my favourite three staff.

'In my own strength I still have no liking for the position as such, but with the Lord's help, I can overcome and can utilize the opportunities.'

For further thought:
1. One of the signs of God's leading is often our desire to do a particular job. But sometimes the call is to an unattractive career. Philippians 2:12–18 is relevant. How can we know whether our dislike of a certain course is merely cowardice or a sign of God's guidance away from it?
2. Many jobs in which Christians find themselves are arduous, tedious and unglamorous. Philippians 4:10–13 suggests that we may need to stay with the problems rather than run away from them. How can we really be *content*? On the other hand, a deep discontent might be a sign that God is moving us on to something else. How can we know?

3. In practical terms, how organized should we be? Think of examples: lists of priorities, prayer lists, set times for prayer and study, completing one task before beginning the next, etc. Does this depend on personality or necessity?

9

Boiling bits of God's world
Robert Newport

Robert is doing research in solid state physics for a PhD at Leicester University. Solid state physics covers both liquids and solids, and Bob is particularly concerned with liquid metals, metals taken up to a high temperature, which means that all his experiments are conducted inside a furnace and in special atmospheres.

Various problems emerge for him as a Christian and a scientist; the need to assure others that he is a useful member of society, for example, when the results of his work may not help anyone for years; the fact that he is working more with things than with people; the conflict that could possibly be seen between rational thought and a belief in God.

We talked around these topics and began with what he was actually working on. What was he trying to prove in his job?

A PhD course is relatively short, three years in fact, and in that time one can do little more than gather information. However, one possible development from my work would be the production of a thermoelectric generator which gives electricity from heat.

A second facet of my work concerns liquid (or molten) semi-conductors. Solid semi-conductors are used in most modern electrical equipment from washing machines to computers. The advantages of a *liquid* semi-conductor are that they might be used in apparatus at a very high temperature, and even in nuclear reactors, as they are not damaged by high radiation levels. But I should emphasize that I am concerned with the investigation, not the future application.

What motivates you for doing a PhD? The end result?

Or a pleasant three years when you can please yourself?

No, it certainly is not those three years. It can still be harder than the undergraduate course. But it's not the end result either. I think it really is the enjoyment of doing it, the day to day enjoyment. Very often you feel as though you are beating your head against a brick wall, but if you look back after three, four or five months' work, you see that you've produced things that no-one else has seen before and you've done them by your own initiative. It's quite rewarding.

How do you adapt to the self-discipline that you must need to get anything done? No-one's going to say you clock in at 9.00 a.m.

Yes, that's right. Really I think a lot of it you learn as an undergraduate, because you are then in almost the same situation, when you have targets like exams and so on to work towards. You've already learnt the attitude required. I think it varies from person to person. Some people drop out very quickly after beginning a PhD because they don't like the life. In fact the drop-out rate in some subjects is as much as 50%; but I find it quite easy to settle down to it.

Why did you choose to do research?

That was very difficult. Obviously I spent a great deal of time in prayer and in talking to people to get their opinions and so on, because it's quite an important decision. In the end what I did was to apply for several things and essentially wait to see which door God left open and which door he closed. I just trusted that he would lead me along the right way as I put my foot forward.

So, Bob, you really are very much involved with *things*; **in particular your liquid metal. How far is this right as a Christian?**

Well, people have to live in this universe which is made up of materials and the Bible says that God created it all and he created it all with order. I must say I find it most fascinating just delving into this universe which God has created. The intricacies are really marvellous.

But how useful is it?

Well, it's not directly related to anything. I hope that later

93

my findings will link up with those of others and the results will be applied in industry. But I must say that that doesn't really worry me too much.

Would it still be valuable as a career?

I think so. A research scientist's career is quite short, rather like that of a footballer. The actual research output tends to drop very rapidly after your mid to late thirties and you then tend to go through to administration, or you direct those below you in doing their research and so on.

Is that because your mind becomes less able or because you want more money?

No, it's not necessarily money; it's mainly because you tend to get into a rut as far as your thinking is concerned. Your thinking patterns have formed and you're not able to cope with new ideas coming along, although there are notable exceptions.

But then experience counts for a lot, doesn't it?

Yes, that's why these older scientists tend to go into directorships of research groups and they can then give a co-ordinated pattern of research to those below them.

Doing research, Bob, you're obviously not as much in contact with people as, say, a sales assistant in a shop. Can it be presumed that you don't have as many relationship difficulties as others?

Not at all. I'm involved with a whole spectrum of people, right from those that are the intellectual 'cream' as it were, to the undergraduates that I teach from time to time, the technicians, the people in the workshop and so on. There is a whole range of people involved and they all have to work together. A Christian has to face all the usual problems, for example the problem of the so-called 'perks'. You want your television mended. You don't take it to a dealer; you bring it here and you get someone to mend it with parts from the stores. There's quite a temptation to go along with that sort of thing.

You talk about being with the intellectual 'cream' and we must accept that some are given more intellect than others by God. But we read how Paul tells that by the foolishness of preaching men are saved. Do you find that being amongst the intellectuals causes problems?

94

Not really, no; I think in some ways it's an advantage. Paul also talks about the membership of the church being like a body with different parts. I think that those who are able to look at things and take them apart in an intellectual way have a part to play in the church, a constructive part to play.

Do you yourself take a part in some local church?

Yes, my wife and I are both members of an evangelical church in Leicester and we have been now for two or three years since we left university.

Quite often the only jobs in a church that are offered are concerned with teaching the young. Have you avoided that trap?

I haven't so much avoided it as answered it. I mean I was approached at one point to help with the Sunday School but I just felt that it wasn't the right thing for me to do; not because I didn't have the material in my mind but because I'm just not gifted to teach children, and if I'd gone in and tried I probably would have bored them stiff. But my wife and I are both involved in a youth group at the church, which we find much more rewarding.

David Field quotes the view that work is a dark tunnel between Sundays when you can do the Lord's work. How would you comment on that?

Well, I disagree almost entirely because I really enjoy my work. It's interesting in itself. Had I not been a Christian I think I would still have been interested in the work I'm doing, but being a Christian sheds a different light on it. You now know whose universe you are looking into so certainly it's no dark tunnel, I thoroughly enjoy it.

I suppose some people still talk about the difficulties for a scientist in being a Christian. They bring up the hoary chestnuts of Genesis 1 and 2. Does that still happen?

Yes it does. Not so much now; it's rather disappointing. I had almost looked forward to these arguments, but a lot of people now seem apathetic and they really don't care one way or the other. Genesis does come up; it comes up quite often whenever there is a discussion. But people are discussing more often whether a religious belief is justified at all, or whether we should treat ourselves as machines, plodding through a very mechanistic universe and eventually turning into other sorts of chemicals. That's the sort of discussion that comes up more frequently. I've really been surprised by the apathy more than anything among these people.

Do you think that, amongst the scientists that you meet, some are prompted to question the origins of the universe?

Well, I sometimes wonder. They seem to live in a very strange dichotomy. At one point they assume that the universe is uniform and orderly, so that if they prove something one day it's going to stay the same tomorrow and for ever, and on the other hand they have this attitude that really the universe is almost imaginary. It doesn't really matter whether there is any order in the universe or not; it's accidental. Maybe another accident can happen and overturn everything. It's a very strange situation and people generally are not prepared to talk about it.

In America it appears to be different, if we can view the attitude of the astronauts as typical. Didn't they read part of the Bible when they arrived on the moon?

Yes, I was quite impressed with that actually, but there are Christians who are scientists in this country and maybe, if we had a space programme, a British Christian would have got to the moon. But the whole of America does seem more alive to these questions.

Are there some areas of scientific method that you are unhappy about as a Christian? I was thinking in terms of experiments on animals, for example.

We are doing things which I am rather concerned over. It's not so much the experimentation on animals, more the commercial attitude, the sort of greed that gets in, for example where cosmetics are tested on animals. Animals are put in our care by God. We are supposed to tend the world we are in, not ravage it. If the experimentation is carried out well, and by and large it is; if you are pursuing research that isn't done for any monetary gain, then there is no incentive to maltreat animals or rush things through or anything like that. It is really when this commercial greed gets in that things start going wrong and I'm very unhappy with that, as most people are.

How far do you regard yourself as a scientist as a different sort of being? Perhaps we have built up an aura around the word.

Yes, it has tended to cloak itself in holy orders almost. Yet scientists *are* different in some respects in that the work they do involves thinking in certain sorts of ways. You rely on the order in the universe and so you have to approach it in an orderly way. You have to think about it in a rational way. The danger, of course, is to confuse your rational thought processes with being a rationalist and excluding God from being the creator and sustainer.

Then you notice other people's irrationalities, their illogicalities?

Well, yes and no. I mean I'd notice fellow scientists' irrationalities because that's something I'm trained to think about, but not in general conversation. A scientist, to be a scientist, has to master this way of thinking or has to be gifted to think this way. Therefore there is a barrier between those who can approach science in that way and those who can't. That means that the education, if you like, of the non-scientist to scientific things becomes very difficult, because you have to bridge that gap somehow.

'I must say I find it most fascinating just delving into this universe which God has created. The intricacies are really marvellous.'

For further thought:

1. Is it right for a Christian to be working with *things* rather than concentrating on *people*? In biblical times, perhaps the priests and rabbis were the only men not to be involved with things in their daily work.

2. Think of other examples of using 'perks' like not paying for one's TV set to be repaired. How can the Christian draw the line without causing bitterness? Have Christians the task

of exposing fraud and denouncing all evil of this kind; or just keeping out of it themselves?

3. When people argue that mankind is just a random collection of particles with no purpose, how can we argue? Do Psalm 8 and Genesis 1-3 help?

10

People come first
Robert Holman

Robert works for the Church of England Children's Society in Bath.
The days when a man could aim for nothing better than following his
father's profession, and getting into a good job for life, have gone. The
socially accepted pattern is to move from job to job, possibly in the same
profession, but possibly into allied fields.

Robert Holman has worked in various different posts, but all in the
field of the social services. First of all, after training, he was a child
care officer in Hertfordshire, involved in receiving children into public
care, finding foster homes and adoptive homes, supervising them in the
homes, and working towards returning them to their parents.

Subsequently he became a professor.

Now he's back in social service.

I asked him how, as a Christian, he had been guided through this
extraordinary set of circumstances.

How did you choose your career in the first place?

I've always been involved in youth club work. I also had
two years in the forces to think things over. I then got involved
with quite a lot of youngsters and in fact did a short spell in a
children's home. This made up my mind for me.

But then you moved over to the more academic side.
Did you want to keep the problems at arm's length?

I'd never thought of leaving social work, although I'd always had a yen to do research. In fact while I was in the children's social work I did carry out one or two small projects
which I then wrote up. But then one day some blurb came
through the door advertising a post at the university. I threw
it in the waste-paper basket and then, when I was transferring

the waste-paper basket to the dustbin, the letter fell out, and in it was a hand-written letter from the person at the university. My old professor had recommended me for a lectureship. Honestly, I was quite astounded by this. I didn't think he'd even noticed my existence. So I thought, if he likes me, perhaps I have got something. That was really the start of it.

So you eventually became a professor of social administration. But that's not what you're doing now.

I'm now a community worker. I'm employed by the Church of England Children's Society and I work almost exclusively on a council estate in Bath.

Did you see your work and 'the Lord's work' as separate fields?

It wasn't so much 'work' and 'the Lord's work', it was the application of Christian teaching to my whole way of living, thinking through what my attitude should be towards materialism, towards neighbours, indeed towards my own career. I had to sort through the social implications of being a Christian and that really was an alarming, fairly painful process.

How does this work out for you in your present post?

When I gave up the Chair at the university this caused some surprise, particularly as I'd been in academic life for about eleven years. You see I wasn't finding the job professionally satisfying, because there was a kind of embargo on development at that time, at the university, and I couldn't expand in the way I wanted to. Further, I felt that for ten years I'd been telling people how to do social work and I wasn't doing it myself. I felt hypocritical; I got out of touch, and I felt if I didn't get out of it now I never would. But there was a second reason. It was this question of life-style. I felt I was living the life of an affluent university professor and one who made a speciality of studying poverty. I lived in a middle-class residential area, with all the trappings of materialism, but that just seemed completely at odds with New Testament Christianity. I wanted to apply New Testament Christianity to my whole life-style as far as I could.

Does this mean then that all professors should change their life-style radically?

No; but for *me*, at this stage in my life, I didn't think I could resolve the question by continuing in my immediate post. Also as a person professionally qualified in social work, I thought that if I had anything to give, it ought to be given in that field at a practical level. I managed to get some funds to put up a community work project and the Church of England Children's Society agreed to employ me for three years. I've moved house within Bath and live on the edge of a council estate where I work.

You rub shoulders with many folk who could be termed 'working class'. Do you think the churches' attitude to them is as it should be?

This is delicate ground in a way because if anyone says that the church is out of touch with working-class people it does cause a lot of resentment. But one of the main issues in my life is the belief that the church is a middle-class institution. Indeed, I'd even say that in many ways people use Christianity to justify or to rationalize middle-class values and materialism.

But don't you think, when people become Christians, they often want to realize their own full potential and therefore better themselves?

Now I think that's a false distinction. I don't think we should ever be opposed to people bettering themselves. Indeed I think that's very much a working-class value, but I think the trouble with people who better themselves is that they become a kind of cut-off elite, separate from the mainstream of society. You know one of the wonderful things about Jesus is that he was working-class but he mixed with people from all grades of life. Jesus was at home, it seems, with the rich young ruler, and also with the paupers and the beggars. There seems to be this mix in the New Testament. This is one of the great things about Christianity. I think we've lost that.

Now what makes the distinction of classes? Is it the type of work that people do or is it the type of upbringing or the culture they know? Is it just because some may be doing more manual work at the factory than others or is it because their parents before them were always doing it?

Well there's no doubt we have a society which is class-ridden. There again, wherever you say this, especially in Christian circles, people resent it. Even Fred Catherwood in his book says he doesn't like to talk about class and to talk about it serves no useful purpose.[1] But it is a major sociological fact that people live different styles of life and that in Britain resources are distributed extremely unequally. The other thing is that because one talks about class it doesn't mean to say that one is a Marxist or a left wing socialist. It just means that one accepts a class analysis as a useful way of looking at society. We've developed a class society and where we live shows this, whether in council estates or in surburban houses . . .

Often those who live in council houses might be doing a manual job and getting more money than the poor professionals.

That's true of course, although if you look at figures you find that very few manual workers do earn higher wages. It's the minority who get in the paper with their Jaguars parked in the council estate; but of course the other point is that a manual worker's wages are at a peak in his twenties and then go down, whereas the professional person's goes up through increments.

What do you think Christians should be doing practically?

I'm not trying to lay down a certain way of life for all Christians. All I'm trying to say is how I worked out my application of Christianity to my life. Coming back to the church issue, it is a factor with many of the youngsters I work with, that they do not like church. They may turn up to church once or twice but then would not go again because they feel uncomfortable there.

You can understand it. It's a foreign place with a ritual they don't know.

Yes, you sing 18th-century hymns and stand up and sit down in certain places and they may even tell you off if you don't wear a suit.

Now in your work how far do you feel it right to talk

[1] Sir Frederick Catherwood, *A better way* (IVP, 1975), p. 41.

about the Lord Jesus when the subject comes up? Do you make opportunities for this?

I dislike the attitude to witness that as a Christian you have got to go round hovering for an opportunity to talk about Christ. It seems to me that Christianity is demonstrated through attitudes and through the way you live and how you respond to a crisis or irritation. So that's the first point I want to make. But in regard to our employment, I think we've got to ask 'what are we paid to do?' In my job I'm paid to try to stop children coming into care or before the courts. It seems to me that if one of the ways of doing that is helping them to understand the Christian faith or to experience the Christian faith, then that's acceptable. I do have the advantage of working for the Church of England Children's Society.

Was it different when you were in social work for the local authority?

Yes, then I took the usual line that I never raised the subject of religion unless people raised it with me. But in my present post I get many opportunities. For instance I'm running a youth club on the estate. We're going away on holiday this year and we decided to go to Butlins at Filey where it's run by Christians. Now all the kids know this but they are still going. Even today I've been with a family and taken them down to the 'nick' to visit their father. You see, because I'm here, and our church is here, I've been talking to them about Sunday school. Again today I've spoken to a chap who lives three doors away from another young man who is converted, wonderfully converted, and just because they are neighbours I was able to say 'it's great isn't it, what's happened to him'. He said to me, 'Yes, when I moved here I had some trouble from him, and I was going to beat him up, but then I saw that he was different now so I'm not going to do it'. So all the time it is give and take because I'm in an area where I go to church and people know I go there.

With your work being so demanding do you have any time or energy at all to give in any specific way in the church? Do you have any, what people might call 'Christian' work?

I run the JUCOs, Junior Covenanters, at our church. We have about 25-30 boys in the group. But there again this work/Christian work distinction is blurred as many of the lads come from around the streets where I live and some of them I see in the course of my job. The whole thing seems to merge into one. As to this question 'what is work and what is not?' I know the two extremes. I know that when I'm away on holiday with my family I'm not working. When I go into the office to dictate some letters, I know I'm working. But then what about when I'm at home playing with my children and two of the boys I've been working with come round and we all start playing together? Here's another example. I went down to our local shop, which is clearly not work, but a storekeeper there told me of someone who had tried to commit suicide. I talked with him. Was that work? It doesn't worry me if it's work or not.

So your vocation, life and work are one whole.
Yes, that about sums it up.

'When I gave up the Chair at the university this caused some surprise . . . as a person professionally qualified in social work, I thought that if I had anything to give, it ought to be given in that field at a practical level.'

For further thought:
1. What are the major social implications of being a Christian? Have we any right to comfort and security? Matthew 6:25–34 is relevant again.
2. Are the churches sufficiently working-class orientated? If not, what needs to be changed?
3. Robert Holman does not suggest that all professors should follow his example. His leading was for him alone. How far should we follow other people's example? How do we know when it is relevant to us? What was Paul getting at in 1 Corinthians 4:16 and Ephesians 5:1?

11

White-collar workers, unite!

Jim Cannon

I met Jim in a luxurious hotel at the Birmingham National Exhibition Centre. Paying 80p for a pot of tea was an unusual experience for both of us but Jim happened to be there for a two-day conference of union and management representatives. He works in a large computer firm, and describes himself as a computer project manager. I asked him to be more specific.

Well, I've worked in a variety of capacities in the firm, but at the moment I'm involved in the control of the installation of a large computer for a county council. The computer is worth £1½ million, which in fact means that every day that we delay a delivery it costs the company £500, so it's quite important that we get it in on time.

When you're dealing with things costing so much money does it make you want to raise your own personal style of living or does a Christian defence mechanism within urge you to be frugal?

I wouldn't say that I must be frugal, but I'm very strict on expenses. There is tremendous scope for fiddling or 'adjusting' expenses. Of course there are a number of non-Christians who are very strict on something like expenses too. You get used to a certain standard, for instance in the type of hotel you stay at when you are away on business. I suppose you do start comparing costs to a certain extent. In the computer business, you see, the smallest device that we provide probably costs about £15,000, which would buy you a very reasonable house, and it possibly sits there for most of the time unused!

You move around with your job to each of the customers?

At the moment I spend a lot of time travelling around the country between the customers' location, my base office in London and manufacturing plants in Manchester and other parts of the country. I have to make sure that everything is running to time, work out what to do if it's not, and think about long-term plans.

You've been in the firm some time?

I've been in the firm since I left college in 1966.

That's unusual, because many people jump from job to job, often with other firms, every two years or so.

I think there's a lot of that, especially in the computer industry. A lot of people seem to join for the first two or three years after leaving university and, when they've had their basic training, they go off somewhere else. At the same time there are still a number of people who like the relative freedom that you have in the type of environment in which I work. I can still count amongst my friends people who joined the company on the same day as I did. It makes for stability in relationships as well as in work and also loyalty. There is a lot to be said for the loyalty that people have towards a company. I think, in fact, that is one of the reasons I got round to joining the union. It would have been so easy to opt out and say, 'Well I'll pack my bags and go somewhere else'.

When did you join your trade union?

Only eighteen months ago. I joined for two main reasons. The first is because the social climate had changed in the country. There is a tremendous amount of activity amongst white-collar unions now. It was also true, in our firm, that a lot more people were feeling that they were becoming small cogs in a larger and larger wheel. They wanted to put their views forward and there was no reasonable mechanism, other than putting things up the line via your boss, who went to his boss and then to his boss and so on. So that was one reason; the change in social climate. The second was the feeling that some things, such as office accommodation and consultation (or lack of it), were becoming bones of contention, and it was either a question of trying to do something about it or opting out. I'm very much for opting *in*. There was a ground-swell of opinion in favour of forming a union group, and so I joined.

Tell me about the trade union set up.

Well I'm not too familiar with trade unions in general, but I can tell you about my own union. This is ASTMS, the Association of Scientific Technical and Managerial Staffs, a large white-collar trade union. Clive Jenkins, the General Secretary of this union, is well known. We are organized on the basis that individuals are elected to the union and I think that this is typical of all trade unions.

Do they have to be nominated by colleagues?

Yes, in our case there is a monthly branch meeting when members are elected in the same way as the Church of England has a parochial church council meeting and people apply to become members of the electoral roll.

What are the main roles of the union?

In the case of my firm you have basically two types of situation. One is the individual situation. Someone has an individual grievance; someone thinks he ought to be on a different grade or wants compassionate leave, and the company refuses. Then the union is called in as an arbiter and helps him put his case. To be fair, we haven't had many situations like that. Then there are the collective issues such as the ones which hit the headlines, for example discussions on pay, work, conditions. . . . I am personally less concerned about things like that although I think it's fair to say that in these times of inflation, pay is a very important factor. What I would like to see unions, and especially our particular union, involved in, is consultations and involvement in the running of companies.

The Bullock Report on Industrial Democracy is looking forward to employee directors. I think that this will happen, although it is quite some way off. The latest legislation on pensions means that companies and recognized unions have to get together to discuss future plans. Planning agreements, where companies, government and unions discuss and agree on long-term strategy, are likely to increase.

And I suppose this conference is an example of progress in this field.

Yes, this was a session when all representatives of all the trade unions in the company came together, to hear what the company's five-year plans were and to question them.

What do you see as the Christian principles behind a trade union?

It's workers joining together to present a common front for the benefit of all. In essence that's the principle behind trade unions. David Field makes the point too that it's a biblical principle. It is also interesting to note that trade unions were started by Christians with a social conscience in many cases.

You might say that these principles take second or third place in our selfish and money-grabbing society.

Well, I'm afraid that's partly true.

Would you advise people to belong to a trade union?

I believe that it's important for people if they do feel strongly about anything to get stuck in and do something, because if they don't, nothing is going to change. I appreciate the power of prayer and I appreciate that some people, such as the Quakers, believe that that is the right approach, to stay out of something and pray that God will move in a majestic fashion. I must say that I don't share that point of view, and I am much more convinced that the right line is to get involved. That includes joining unions.

Do you believe that you, as an individual, can have much impact?

Yes I do. There are two points that I ought to make in answer to that. The first is that in fact I have only been in the union for a period of eighteen months. The second point is closely tied in with this, that I joined at that time because lots of people were voicing their fears and worries about a whole range of situations and I thought it would be useful to try to provide some sort of direction to this. I was instrumental in pushing the union forward, if you like. The end-product of that is that I am now in a key position and whenever I get involved in discussions, provided I put forward a reasonable line, then people do tend to listen, so the end result is that I believe my views as an individual count. So far I've not had any difficulties, but I think it is not beyond the realms of possibility that I might. Certainly we have the odd discussion at branch meetings about crossing picket lines and I think there could well be cases where I might feel my conscience dictated a course of action against the general line.

Have you ever been in a sticky position in the union, as a Christian? For example, strike action, withholding one's labour?

Yes, the question is, if he finds himself in a minority, should the Christian sink his personal scruples and join in a strike of which he disapproves? My answer is, it depends very much on the particular case. I can see lots of instances where I might disagree with the general view but I should still follow it. I'm not sure what I would do about a fundamental issue, such as a closed shop. It may be that I would oppose the union policy even after it had been agreed. But I think it's worth pointing out that trade unions hit the headlines because of strikes, but so often the strikes are way, way down the list. I really cannot envisage any circumstances under which my group would ever get round to strike action.

Have you personally found Christians prejudiced against unions?

I think people tend to feel that the unions run the country. Actually there is a big split in the trade union movement itself between the right and the left. The left tend to say, 'We want to maintain our independence of management and we want to retain our pristine bargaining rights'; and the moderate view tends to be, 'Let's work together to go forward'. I am in favour of the second approach; working together. I don't believe, in any case, that the unions do run the country. I think, especially in the last two years in fact, that trade unions have had enormously beneficial effects, abiding by the pay policy. I think again that this is a very good case where the Christian point of view can come into its own. My own view is that there is a lot to be said for a wages policy and I relate that to one of my fundamental beliefs that the strong ought to be helping the weak. . . .

Which David Field brings out very strongly as a biblical principle from the Old Testament onwards.

That's right, and that's one of my basic tenets of living the Christian life, that the strong ought to be helping the weak. This applies on a parochial level; it applies on a national level and it applies on an international level, and I think if we don't do that then we are being selfish. I don't always have the support of other members of the union on that, but at least I have the opportunity of putting my point of view.

This is where Christians can be salt.

Well I hope so, I really do hope so. I am not so sure that we always are as salty as we should be. It is very difficult at times to remember the need to be salty, and this is again where David Field's question about following the democratic wishes of the majority comes in and it depends very much on that issue.

In the New Testament we find that Paul gives instructions to employers and employees, slaves to obey their masters, and David Field comments that this would be quite as unpopular an injunction then as it is now.

I think that ties in with his comments on 'give me the right conditions and I will work whole-heartedly with you'. His argument is that the Christian ought not to say that. I don't know that I entirely agree with that. There are absolutely black and white situations in which the Christian is, I would say, entitled to plead that he needs the right conditions. For example, I don't believe it's reasonable to expect people to work in unsafe conditions, and therefore the Christian, the worker, is fully justified in saying, 'unless you do something about this I will not work there'.

Exploitation comes in the same bracket, I suppose?

Yes, I think the good employer wouldn't want to do that anyhow. Again, in the UK at this stage, the laws of the land have so developed that employers are forced to maintain a very much higher standard of health and safety at work than formerly, which I think is all to the good.

How do you think David Field treats the subject of vocation?

Well, he points out that all Christians have a vocation. I believe that there is a tremendous amount of truth in that but at the same time there are shades of grey in working this out in practice. For instance, if I became redundant I would feel obliged to take up employment which may not use my talent to the full, which may not be my line at all. It might be cleaning windows or washing dishes in a restaurant, but I might feel morally obliged to do that in order to support my family.

David Field says that workers with a sense of vocation are inevitably men and women with ambition. He then says that this may be a reason why so few Christians are to be found in unskilled jobs. That is one possible explanation, but there are many others which to my mind are more realistic and I believe that they have a closer bearing on the truth. For example the fact that the church in the United Kingdom is very much a middle-class institution. That in itself builds barriers which need to be removed.

To be honest, I'm not sure that in everything I do I remember that my aim is to serve God. That might sound a terrible admission. When I sit down and write a name or tear a strip off somebody or whatever, I am not consciously thinking, 'I've got to do this well for Jesus'. I just do the best I can. Christianity is more an approach, an underlying attitude.

'It was either a question of trying to do something about it or opting out. I'm very much for opting in. There was a ground-swell of opinion in favour of forming a union group, and so I joined.'

For further thought:
1. Compare Jim's attitude on opting in with Mike Kinch's comments on page 38. What pointers are there for a Christian who wonders whether to join a union or not?
2. Are there any other ways of 'getting involved' rather than joining a union? How best can the Christian be salt and light? Matthew 5:13–16.
3. Jim gives the impression that a Christian should support the 'right wing' unionists who would in fact help the weak by adhering to a pay policy, but not the left wingers who are concerned to dominate. Is this a just summary of his views? Do you agree with them?

12

Art for God's sake
Stephen and Micki Hounslow

Stephen and Michaela live near the centre of St Albans. When I talked to them they had been married only two months and so were adapting to a new life and work pattern. Stephen designs furniture; Micki teaches art four days a week in a school for physically handicapped children.

M: I'm employed to teach art, though quite frequently I am asked to teach other subjects, and I work with children of all ages from nursery age to sixteen.

Have you been trained to teach the handicapped?

M: No, not specifically. I did my training at Art College, with a foundation year followed by a painting course and an art teacher training year. While I was on my final course I did two teaching practices; one in a Comprehensive school in London, the other at the school where I am now teaching. My first teaching practice I found very difficult and I couldn't imagine myself becoming a teacher. But I had prayed about it and felt confident that the Lord wanted me to do the course, so I thought, 'If you want me to teach, then I will'.

During the second half of the course I wondered about trying another form of teaching and thought of special education. While I was on my second teaching practice I was offered my present job.

Are you doing this, as a Christian, because you feel that these kids have greater needs than others, and you can serve better this way?

M: No, not particularly. I feel that this sort of teaching job suits me, but, more important, it's where God has put me.

I enjoy the work and probably have qualities that are suitable for the job. I think I am quite patient with the children. There must be children in other schools whose needs require the sort of abilities which I don't have.

You not only teach; you also paint.

M: Yes. For the past year I've been working a four-day week so that on the fifth day I can devote my time to painting. But since our marriage I haven't done as much painting as I would like.

Do you get absorbed and away from everything else when you're painting?

M: Yes. It does take all my concentration, and I do find it hard work. I can't paint properly if I feel tired. That's one reason why I haven't done so much recently. The emotional adjustments as well as new routines have taken a lot out of me.

Have you ever considered painting as a commercial proposition?

M: Yes. But my painting isn't sufficiently organized at the moment to enable me to sell enough to earn a living from it. Nevertheless, I am doing what I can and we are both trying to find ways of selling my work. Despite the difficulties, I believe that God honours our attempts to use his gifts and he will prosper them as he sees fit.

Stephen, painters in the past have been able to paint *and* live. What is your comment on that?

S: Some painters have always found it difficult to make ends meet: even great painters like Rembrandt have ended their lives in quite considerable poverty. Some have made ends meet by working under the patronage of some great family or the church. There have been certain artists, like Turner, who had a very good grasp of economics as well as of painting, but this seems to be rare in the painting profession.

Are there many full-time painters now?

S: A little while ago somebody reckoned that there were only about six fine artists in the country who actually make a living from their work.

Is artistic vision something that you feel God has put in you to express?

M: Well, I don't think that because you have an artistic gift from God, you also necessarily have a vision. It often seems that as you exercise your gift, your vision is built up through your own work and experience of life. By that I mean that vision is not limited by, or independent of, past experience, effort and discipline. I believe vision has to do with the significance or meaning of what you see. So, for Christians, vision is to be built up through knowledge of God and God's world; it means getting to grips with God's word and getting to know God.

But in other professions, for example, administration, the whole concept of work is different from how an artist sees it. Would you agree?

S: I think that in recent times, society has elevated the artist to a role above that of the ordinary workman. This is a pity. I am not sure that the artist's view of *work* is in any way distinctive. The only thing I can say is that the artist cannot regard his work in a mechanical or detached fashion. He *has* to give himself, his concentration, his powers of ingenuity, probably his emotions, whether conscious or unconscious, and so on. He *has* to take initiative. But in all these things he may not be unique. Perhaps we have alienated the artist from his contemporaries by giving him a sense of importance which he doesn't really possess.

Then it depends on other people, whether they will buy his work. It's with them whether they will make or mar him, isn't it? It's society's problem.

S: Society can only 'make' an artist in the commercial sense. It cannot make an artist 'great' if he is not a great artist; it can only make him *appear* great. In the end an artist must be judged on his work not his reputation.

M: It's not the public at large who decide his reputation anyway. Only a small section of the public are attracted to art galleries. It seems that art for the 'man in the street' is the art of the media, packaging, television, record sleeves, car design, and that Art with a capital 'A' has become so obscure that it lacks meaning for him. Perhaps it is because of this obscurity and mystique that the artist has been elevated to an unreachable position.

Stephen, do you call yourself an artist?

S: Yes, in that I tend to draw my inspiration for a particular job from within myself. Sometimes this inspiration seems to be born out of thought and effort (a sort of trial and error process in which there is a moment of illumination). At other times this inspiration appears more like a revelation 'from out of the blue', although I suspect that neither process is really independent of the other. I am dependent on this process of creativity: of something arising out of myself. This often takes the form of seeing a new relationship or possible relationship between objects or ideas which may be already familiar to me. In this sense, my vocation is creative or artistic. On the other hand I do not consider myself an 'artist' if that removes me from the simple, down-to-earth business of getting my hands dirty. If I divorce myself from the ordinary workman then I am forced to deny a part of myself.

At the moment I am purely involved in designing furniture, although I have also had training and experience as a cabinet-maker. I have just accepted a new post which will again enable me to make, as well as design, furniture.

What do you enjoy about your profession?

S: There are many enjoyments. One is the gathering of an idea in the mind and organizing it into something which can be made, and then seeing the thing made. A second kind of enjoyment is the tactile enjoyment of handling materials, making them fit, and shaping them to form something that wasn't there before.

Do you get the same satisfaction out of painting, Micki?

M: Yes, I do enjoy these satisfactions, and in addition, there's a satisfaction in the calmness produced by having the mind fully concentrated. Part of the incentive to work is the enjoyment of the process of working as much as the end-product.

Stephen you're in a commercial world. There must be pressures. What sort of problems do you come across?

S: There are problems born out of being required to produce an article within a certain time limit. Sometimes this doesn't allow an idea to be developed to the full. There are problems concerning the kind of articles to be produced. Sometimes a client will require an item which doesn't happen to appeal. This is so whether you work for a large company and are dictated to by a marketing team, or whether you work for an individual client. Clashes of taste and personality can easily arise. So far as I can see, this has always been a problem: it was a problem for those under the patronage of the Medici. Somewhere in the middle of all this, the artist often is able to work within these constraints and yet produce something which is very individual. Constraints often produce a clarity of order whereas total licence usually produces confusion.

Is the desire to produce the very best, peculiar to the Christian?

S: It's not exclusive to the Christian; if it were, a lot of fine articles would never have been produced. There is some general sense of the need for perfection.

M: Great art has come from non-Christian cultures; the Japanese for example.

Then can you give anything more because you're a Christian?

S: I think you can. There is a difference in the spirit in which you work. When Jesus said that we must 'be perfect, as your heavenly Father is perfect', I recognize that he was referring to our moral behaviour, but I believe that there is a principle involved, which requires us never to stop short at standards which will satisfy men. There is a need for the Christian to have a high view of the value of work and workmanship. Therefore, he should strive to attain the highest possible standards. The perfection of our Father in heaven, whom we know, must be greater than any other worldly perfection, so our standard must be higher. If a workman is a practising Christian it should be reflected in the consistently high standard of his workmanship.

M: A Christian has a respect for what is truthful in his work. He shouldn't be satisfied merely to produce something that would sell, or gain him a reputation, or pass-mark at college. One has to strive for what is really true.

And still get enough money to live! How far is work the main part of your life?

S: I suppose my 'job' tends to overflow into what one might call leisure time; work on the house for example. There's no clear division. I find within me an intense drive to work. I don't think I could ever be satisfied with a purely leisurely life. My drive always seems to be towards creating something. My college professor once said 'You can turn a man to face any direction you like but he will end up facing the same way'. There's some degree of truth in that when it comes to the man who likes to *make*.

You both work. I know you've only recently embarked on a life together. So we come to the traditional comment that 'the work of the woman is in the home'. How do you feel about that, Micki?

M: We haven't sorted this out completely, but I don't think that a woman loses her respect or is degraded if she takes on the role of the housewife. At the same time I think it's quite acceptable for a woman to have a career. I think it's probably something that has to be worked out between husband and wife, particularly as there are so many false ideas floating around in society. As far as our own life is concerned, we take turns in making the breakfast, although generally I do most of the cooking. We seem to share many of the jobs around the house, because we are both really interested in what the house looks like. However, because I actually *like* cooking, I don't feel that I am being given all the dirty work.

You're both in full-time work, and then there's the house. Are you able to put in any specific 'Christian work'?

S: Up to now we have both been involved in various types of work, both outside and within the church. Part of our work together has been to redecorate the inside of the church as a scheme. As we've just moved to a new district we are not yet fully involved in any regular church work there.

In decorating the church, that would be using the skills, the abilities, the gifts you have in your present paid work.

S: Yes. I feel that there is a very strong need, particularly in the evangelical wing of the church, if I may use that term, for meaningful interiors (and exteriors for that matter); for interiors which have some relation to the mood and practice of the church. A church building is not just a shell in which to perform a duty, but it does have an intrinsic effect on the people who are in it. One would only have to walk into (a) a dungeon, and (b) a palace, to notice some difference in the mood, purpose and significance of the building, the moment one stepped through the door. Therefore I feel it important that we should use positively these aspects of a building.

So you would feel that people who have gifts that they use in their main bread-earning job should also contribute in that way to their local body of believers?

S: I think they can. Obviously each member has his own particular calling and I think we all have a God-arranged contribution to make to the church which may or may not involve the experience of our occupation. I think it is easy to degrade the importance of practical help in the service of the church. If a need is present and we have the skills then why not use them?

M: I believe that if you're willing to be used, God will show you how you can be useful, confirming a task to you.

Let's move over to the idea of vocation. Have you always been in the same profession?

S: I would say I have been in this profession almost as long as I have been alive, if you call my 'profession' making things, but I have only pursued it as a career for the past twelve years.

So how far do we regard it as your vocation?

S: As a Christian, one's vocation is of eternal significance

118

and not just something restricted to a life's work. If it is of eternal significance it is obviously something about which to seek God's guidance; 'What is my vocation?' does not mean 'What is it that I want to do in life?' but 'What does *he* want me to do in life?' It is really *his* vocation as much as *my* vocation, and for my part I am convinced that God has called me to try to fulfil, as much as I can, my capacity to make and create beautiful things, particularly in wood. Because he has called me to do this I believe that both my standards of workmanship and design must be subject to spiritual values. When I look at God's example of design, the world around us, I am aware of a perfect integration of structure and expression on every scale and a perfect interrelation between each scale of structures and expressions. It is a search to find harmony between structure and expression which is a major motivating force in my work. If I am to create in a spiritual way, I am to create with sensitivity and with due regard to the fact that God has made the materials I use.

I wonder how far this is a generally masculine view. What do you think, Micki?

M: My views about vocation are the same in that I feel it is of eternal significance and that the one who does the calling is God and not some feeling within myself. I think the important thing about vocation is that we are obedient in fulfilling the task God has revealed to us at the moment. I realize that I may at some time be called to be a mother and so far as my vocation is concerned that's not second best to being an artist. Neither is being an artist a substitute for being a mother. The two may even go hand in hand.

Do you think at the back of many girls' minds is the thought 'I want something I can opt out of'?

M: To take this view is almost to tell God what vocation would suit me best. I do have a natural desire towards motherhood, but at the moment I know I have been called to be a painter, teacher and wife. There was a time when, in the face of opposition, I wondered if painting was a worth-while thing to pursue, but I believe that God confirmed it by showing me through his word that one day he would taste the fruits of my work. Vocation isn't necessarily the line of least resistance.

It is sometimes regarded that the Lord's work is, for example, teaching or Sunday school work. Work is what you get paid for and you leave behind you with relief and take your salary. How far do you see a distinction between the Lord's work and other work?

S: Because Christ desires that every area of our activity is brought within his rule, or kingdom, it is quite legitimate to speak of the Lord's work as applying to every part of our lives. Perhaps this could be called 'the Lord's work in general'. This should *include* specific acts of remembrance and worship both individual and corporate. Some people refer to the Lord's work as those activities restricted to the proclamation of the gospel and the service of the community of God's people – the church. Others would extend this to include the service of the community in general, specifically in the Lord's name. Maybe these latter views can be referred to as 'the Lord's work in particular'. But it should be remembered that the Bible does not permit us to engage in any activity, paid or unpaid, which is forgetful of God or disobedient to him.

Some evangelism could take place during your paid work. Is this true for you?

M: Yes and no really. There have been opportunities when I have been able to evangelize, but I feel it would be wrong to do so in working time if the job suffered. At the same time, I think that working relationships plus the witness of your approach to your job, help to testify to who you say you are and what you believe. In my own experience God *does* open up opportunities and will even create a desire to speak to someone *just* when they are ready to receive it, provided I am willing to be used.

Do you have similar opportunities, Steve, at work?

S: Yes. I think there are always opportunities if you are willing to use them. I think you have to bear in mind that whatever the job, you are usually working with people and that there's not only the witness of the way the job is done, there's the witness of the way you get on with other people. If you're seen to be somebody who's patient, someone who is forbearing and trustworthy, I think these are the sort of qualities which people respect even if they have no concept of God. You can't work with someone who is not trustworthy; you can with someone who is. I think that if you are going to speak about your faith in any really convincing way then you have almost to earn this right to speak by the way in which you carry yourself and the way you do your job. It would seem highly unconvincing for someone to speak to me about their knowledge of Christ if they bore no particular witness in their personality or the way they worked.

Micki, you're teaching four days a week. How secure is your job?

M: It is probably less secure now with the current situation in the teaching profession. The head of my school has already informed the staff of a possible cutback in teachers, and as I am a part-time specialist teacher my job is perhaps less secure than those of my colleagues.

How do you feel about that then?

M: I am keeping my eyes open for another job and I believe God will provide another situation if he wants me to move.

I could say, well it's easy for you because if you lose your job you've always got your husband to support you.

M: It doesn't seem to be a responsible attitude simply to rely upon the financial support of your husband unless it is necessary or is an agreed plan.

Stephen, are you ambitious?

S: I am very ambitious to attain high standards in my work. I have always believed that if you are doing your present job as unto the Lord, even though the task in hand may be boring or frustrating, in some way the Lord will protect your position. One verse which was a great help to me, when I was in a particularly dull situation, was that which says that promotion comes neither from the east nor from the west but from the Lord. I think that this is true for every Christian. He is the only true source of promotion.

'There is a need for the Christian to have a high view of the value of work and workmanship. Therefore, he should strive to attain the highest possible standards. . . . If a workman is a practising Christian it should be reflected in the consistently high standard of his workmanship.'

For further thought:
1. What is implied in the pursuit of high standards of workmanship? Voluntary overtime? Unpopularity with colleagues? Accusations of worldly ambition? Is compromise sometimes necessary? See Ephesians 6:5–8.
2. Is art of any use? Is there a Christian argument for it?
3. For a Christian, does vocation have an 'eternal significance'? If so, how and why?

Postscript

So the package is unpacked. And what have we found?

Certainly nothing so clear-cut as a computer print-out definition of Christian vocation. Reading through these chapters, one does not see any signs of a formidable strait-jacket labelled 'Vocation', into which thirteen very different people have tried to cramp the aching limbs of their working lives, doing their best to grin and bear it because they are Christians. Instead of that, a refreshing air of flexibility, freedom and even exhilaration breathes through all the interviews.

Putting this book together has been a risky business. Part 1 has been written by a middle-aged clergyman living in the ivory tower of a theological college. Part 2 has been compiled largely from interviews with thirteen men and women who are immersed in the ordinary workaday world. Both parts attempt to relate the Bible's teaching to real-life Christian working experience. But how could they ever be made to fit?

Naturally, there are differences of interpretation and outlook. Jim Cannon questions my conclusion that no Christian should say 'Give me the right conditions, *then* I will work whole-heartedly'. Elspeth Stephenson takes me to task for failing to consider the married woman's work-load. The contributors sometimes disagree among themselves, on the rights and wrongs of taking part in trade union activities, for example. But over and above the differences, and across the boundaries of sex, class and age, an impressive unity emerges.

I noticed three things in particular.

1. An integrated approach to life

Many of those who spoke to Elspeth Stephenson showed a marked reluctance to confine their view of vocation to their paid job or to any other particular department of life. As a result, several common distinctions become a little blurred. In his life as a community worker, for example, Robert Holman finds it hard to define the boundary between his job and his unpaid 'Christian work'. To use his own words, 'the whole thing seems to merge into one'. Along with several other contributors, he also finds the dividing line between work and leisure hard to distinguish at times. How indeed do you describe Gillian Wilson-Dickson's *vocation*, when she looks after her children and home for nothing as her top priority, and gets paid for giving concerts, which she regards as her recreation and hobby?

Michael Coupe finds the answer lies in focusing on *being* rather than *doing*. That, for him, is the start of a Christian solution to redundancy. Jim Cannon agrees with the general principle. At work as in everything else, he says, living as a Christian is 'more an approach, an underlying attitude'.

This surely reflects an important biblical truth. In the New Testament, the purpose of God's calling (which is what vocation is all about) is expressed far more often in terms of quality of life than of work and occupation. Peter and Paul, for example, tell their readers that God is calling them to be holy, patient and worthy people.[1] Only once (and then only marginally) does Paul link God's calling with jobs.[2] This is not to say that God has no plan for his people's careers. But it does underline the point that his primary call is for Christians to *be* his people in the whole of their lives, including the hours they spend at work.

The same note is struck in the Old Testament. It was the Jews' pagan neighbours who divided their lives into compartments, with a separate deity in charge of each section. God taught his people differently. They were to live the whole of their lives under the all-enveloping canopy of his will. God's

[1] 1 Corinthians 1:2; 1 Peter 2:20–21; 2 Thessalonians 1:11.
[2] 1 Corinthians 7:17.

calling embraced everything they were and all that they did, whether at worship, at work or in their leisure pursuits. The umbrella of vocation did not extend to just one isolated patch of life called 'work'. It stretched out to cover everything in an integrated whole.

2. A flexible view of vocation

Even when used in its narrower sense (to mean a job of work), vocation is not a word that can apply only to a select few 'Christian' occupations, while everything else must be labelled an 'ordinary job'. All thirteen contributors are sure about that. Can a bricklayer's labourer call his work 'vocational'? Michael Kinch has no doubt at all. 'It's all the Lord's work. I just live for the Lord.' And as a manager, John Kinder agrees from the other side of the industrial divide. God can call people to do an infinite variety of jobs, and each one is as much a vocation as any other.

Do we just occasionally catch a faint echo of the opposite point of view, the feeling that some occupations are more worth-while than others, in Christian eyes, if not in God's? 'My work may not be directly for the glory of God', admits John Kinder, 'as if I were standing up at the roadside, preaching.' Robin Keeley contrasts the 'very spiritual' work of teaching and counselling with the paperwork waiting for him on his vicarage desk. And Gillian Wilson-Dickson illustrates the same reactions in reverse. To her, looking after the home and family is 'far more the Lord's work than anything "churchy"'.

Perhaps this is a nettle we must grasp more firmly. God's calling may take individuals into very different occupations. But when we can't get rid of the idea that it is more valuable to do some things in this life than others, are we stating an important general truth about vocation, or just reflecting the way *we* are being called and led personally?

Several of the interviews illustrate one important corollary of a flexible view of vocation. It is only to be expected that God will call some people to change their jobs, perhaps many times, while he wants others to continue in the same occupation for life. This is not just a modern idea. It is thoroughly biblical.

Farming was just as much part of Amos' total vocation, for example, as prophecy. When the change came, it only marked a bend in the road of God's calling, not the beginning of his vocation.

3. A positive approach to work

This is surely the most persistent note struck through all twelve chapters of Part 2. In days when it is unfashionable to admit that you enjoy your job, even if you do, it comes as all the more of a surprise to hear men and women talking about their work in terms of satisfaction and enjoyment. Once or twice I found myself wondering whether more interviewees might have been found with jobs everyone could immediately recognize as dismally dull and boring. But on closer reading the answer lies deeper than that.

For one thing, there is a refreshing strain of honesty in all the contributions. As Mary Hemes has discovered in her school staff-room, and as Michael Kinch finds every time he has to fight for a hose-pipe on his building site, being a Christian at work can create problems as well as solve them. Robert Newport tells of pressures to accept perks in his job, a problem which presumably troubles only those with tender consciences.

So how can Christians substantiate their claim to find some kind of positive 'faith extra' in their attitude to work? For our contributors, it is obviously the God-centred approach that does it. God is in everything. John Marsh the surgeon sees him at work behind the suture needle and in the moulds that provide the antibiotics. Mary Hemes has found his strength available and adequate to cope with crises in the class-room. For Michael Coupe, it is God who makes sense of redundancy. To John Kinder he provides worthwhile objectives, and to Robert Newport he gives clear guidance. And so one might go on. In the experience of everyone interviewed, God's presence and control make a crucial difference to the way they look at their work.

This provides us with the key to understanding vocation at its most basic. The word itself is a passive one. Strictly speaking, it is meaningless to speak of 'choosing my vocation'. Every vocation is initiated by God. As Elspeth Stephenson so rightly reminds us, God wants no sleeping partners who 'sit on their backsides and let the world flow around them'. But he is still the Prime Mover. It is he who calls, and the words, 'I will' mark the human starting-point of every vocation. Let Stephen and Micki Hounslow have the last word: ' "What is my vocation?" does not mean "What is it that I want to do in life?" but "What does *he* want me to do in life?" . . . I think the most important thing about vocation is that we are obedient in fulfilling the task God has revealed to us at the moment.'

'He who calls you is faithful' (1 Thessalonians 5:24).